The Poetry of Bliss Carman

Volume XIX - Later Poems

William Bliss Carman was born in Fredericton, in New Brunswick on April 15th 1861. He was educated at Fredericton Collegiate School before moving to the University of New Brunswick, obtaining his B.A. there in 1881. As is common with so many writers his first published piece was for the University magazine and for Carman that was in 1879.

After several years editing various magazines and periodicals Carman first published a poetry volume in 1893 with Low Tide on Grand Pré. There was no Canadian company prepared to publish and when an American company did so it went bankrupt.

The following year was decidedly better. His partnership with the American poet Richard Hovey had given birth to Songs of Vagabondia. It was an immediate success.

That success prompted the Boston firm, Stone & Kimball, to reissue Low Tide on Grand Pré and to hire Carman as the editor of its literary journal, The Chapbook.

Carman brought out, in 1895, Behind the Arras, a somewhat more serious and philosophical work centered on the premise of a long meditation, using the speaker's house and its many rooms, as a symbol of life and the choices to be made.

In 1896 Carman met Mrs Mary Perry King, who rapidly became patron, adviser and sometime lover. She also became his writing collaborator on two verse dramas.

In 1897 Carman published Ballad of Lost Haven, and in 1898, By the Aurelian Wall, the title poem itself was an elegy to John Keats and the book was a collection of formal elegies.

As the century turned Carman was hard at work on a five-volume set of poetry "Pans Pipes". The excellence of a number of these poems did much to install Carman as the most noted of Canadian Poets and eventually their own Poet Laureate.

In 1912 the final work in the Vagabondia series was published. Richard Hovey had died in 1900 and so this last work was purely Carman's. It has a distinct elegiac tone as if remembering the past works themselves.

On October 28th, 1921 Carman was honored by the newly-formed Canadian Authors' Association where he was crowned Canada's Poet Laureate with a wreath of maple leaves.

William Bliss Carman died of a brain hemorrhage at the age of 68 in New Canaan on the 8th June, 1929.

Oh, well the world is dreaming
Under the April moon,
Her soul in love with beauty,
Her senses all a-swoon!

Pure hangs the silver crescent
Above the twilight wood,
And pure the silver music
Wakes from the marshy flood.

O Earth, with all thy transport,
How comes it life should seem
A shadow in the moonlight,
A murmur in a dream?

Index of Contents
VESTIGIA
A REMEMBRANCE
THE SHIPS OF YULE
THE SHIPS OF SAINT JOHN
THE GARDEN OF DREAMS
GARDEN MAGIC
IN GOLD LACQUER
APRILIAN
GARDEN SHADOWS
IN THE DAY OF BATTLE
TREES
THE GIVERS OF LIFE
A FIRESIDE VISION
A WATER COLOR
THRENODY FOR A POET
DUST OF THE STREET
TO A YOUNG LADY ON HER BIRTHDAY
THE GIFT
THE CRY OF THE HILLBORN
A MOUNTAIN GATEWAY
MORNING IN THE HILLS
A WOODPATH
WEATHER OF THE SOUL
HERE AND NOW
THE ANGEL OF JOY
THE HOMESTEAD
"THE STARRY MIDNIGHT WHISPERS"
A LYRIC
"APRIL NOW IN MORNING CLAD"
NIKE
THE ENCHANTED TRAVELLER
SPRING'S SARABAND
TRIUMPHALIS
"NOW THE LENGTHENING TWILIGHTS HOLD"

THE SOUL OF APRIL
AN APRIL MORNING
EARTH VOICES
RESURGAM
EASTER EVE
NOW IS THE TIME OF YEAR
THE REDWING
THE RAINBIRD
LAMENT
UNDER THE APRIL MOON
THE FLUTE OF SPRING
SPRING NIGHT
BLOODROOT
DAFFODIL'S RETURN
NOW THE LILAC TREE'S IN BUD
WHITE IRIS
THE TREE OF HEAVEN
PEONY
THE URBAN PAN
THE SAILING OF THE FLEETS
"'TIS MAY NOW IN NEW ENGLAND"
IN EARLY MAY
FIREFLIES
THE PATH TO SANKOTY
OFF MONOMOY
IN ST GERMAIN STREET
PAN IN THE CATSKILLS
A NEW ENGLAND JUNE
THE TENT OF NOON
CHILDREN OF DREAM
ROADSIDE FLOWERS
THE GARDEN OF SAINT ROSE
THE WORLD VOICE
SONGS OF THE GRASS
THE CHORISTERS
THE WEED'S COUNSEL
THE BLUE HERON
WOODLAND RAIN
SUMMER STORM
DANCE OF THE SUNBEAMS
THE CAMPFIRE OF THE SUN
SUMMER STREAMS
THE GOD OF THE WOODS
AT SUNRISE
AT TWILIGHT
MOONRISE
THE QUEEN OF NIGHT
NIGHT LYRIC

THE HEART OF NIGHT
PEACE
THE OLD GRAY WALL
TE DEUM
IN OCTOBER
BY STILL WATERS
LINES FOR A PICTURE
THE DESERTED PASTURE
AUTUMN
NOVEMBER TWILIGHT
THE GHOSTYARD OF THE GOLDENROD
BEFORE THE SNOW
WINTER
A WINTER PIECE
WINTER STREAMS
WINTER TWILIGHT
THE TWELFTH NIGHT STAR
A CHRISTMAS EVE CHORAL
CHRISTMAS SONG
THE WISE MEN FROM THE EAST
THE SENDING OF THE MAGI
THE ANGELS OF MAN
AT THE MAKING OF MAN
ST. MICHAEL'S STAR
THE DREAMERS
EL DORADO
ON THE PLAZA
A PAINTER'S HOLIDAY
MIRAGE
THE WINGED VICTORY
THE GATE OF PEACE
EPILOGUE
BLISS CARMAN – AN APPRECIATION
BLISS CARMAN – A SHORT BIOGRAPHY
BLISS CARMAN – A CONCISE BIBLIOGRAPHY

LATER POEMS

Vestigia

I took a day to search for God,
And found Him not. But as I trod
By rocky ledge, through woods untamed,
Just where one scarlet lily flamed,
I saw His footprint in the sod.

Then suddenly, all unaware,

Far off in the deep shadows, where
A solitary hermit thrush
Sang through the holy twilight hush—
I heard His voice upon the air.

And even as I marvelled how
God gives us Heaven here and now,
In a stir of wind that hardly shook
The poplar leaves beside the brook—
His hand was light upon my brow.

At last with evening as I turned
Homeward, and thought what I had learned
And all that there was still to probe—
I caught the glory of His robe
Where the last fires of sunset burned.

Back to the world with quickening start
I looked and longed for any part
In making saving Beauty be....
And from that kindling ecstasy
I knew God dwelt within my heart.

A Remembrance

Here in lovely New England
When summer is come, a sea-turn
Flutters a page of remembrance
In the volume of long ago.

Soft is the wind over Grand Pré,
Stirring the heads of the grasses,
Sweet is the breath of the orchards
White with their apple-blow.

There at their infinite business
Of measuring time forever,
Murmuring songs of the sea,
The great tides come and go.

Over the dikes and the uplands
Wander the great cloud shadows,
Strange as the passing of sorrow,
Beautiful, solemn, and slow.

For, spreading her old enchantment

Of tender ineffable wonder,
Summer is there in the Northland!
How should my heart not know?

The Ships of Yule

When I was just a little boy,
Before I went to school,
I had a fleet of forty sail
I called the Ships of Yule;

Of every rig, from rakish brig
And gallant barkentine,
To little Fundy fishing boats
With gunwales painted green.

They used to go on trading trips
Around the world for me,
For though I had to stay on shore
My heart was on the sea.

They stopped at every port to call
From Babylon to Rome,
To load with all the lovely things
We never had at home;

With elephants and ivory
Bought from the King of Tyre,
And shells and silk and sandal-wood
That sailor men admire;

With figs and dates from Samarcand,
And squatty ginger-jars,
And scented silver amulets
From Indian bazaars;

With sugar-cane from Port of Spain,
And monkeys from Ceylon,
And paper lanterns from Pekin
With painted dragons on;

With cocoanuts from Zanzibar,
And pines from Singapore;
And when they had unloaded these
They could go back for more.

And even after I was big
And had to go to school,
My mind was often far away
Aboard the Ships of Yule.

The Ships of Saint John

Where are the ships I used to know,
That came to port on the Fundy tide
Half a century ago,
In beauty and stately pride?

In they would come past the beacon light,
With the sun on gleaming sail and spar,
Folding their wings like birds in flight
From countries strange and far.

Schooner and brig and barkentine,
I watched them slow as the sails were furled,
And wondered what cities they must have seen
On the other side of the world.

Frenchman and Britisher and Dane,
Yankee, Spaniard and Portugee,
And many a home ship back again
With her stories of the sea.

Calm and victorious, at rest
From the relentless, rough sea-play,
The wild duck on the river's breast
Was not more sure than they.

The creatures of a passing race,
The dark spruce forests made them strong,
The sea's lore gave them magic grace,
The great winds taught them song.

And God endowed them each with life—
His blessing on the craftsman's skill—
To meet the blind unreasoned strife
And dare the risk of ill.

Not mere insensate wood and paint
Obedient to the helm's command,
But often restive as a saint
Beneath the Heavenly hand.

All the beauty and mystery
Of life were there, adventure bold,
Youth, and the glamour of the sea
And all its sorrows old.

And many a time I saw them go
Out on the flood at morning brave,
As the little tugs had them in tow,
And the sunlight danced on the wave.

There all day long you could hear the sound
Of the caulking iron, the ship's bronze bell,
And the clank of the capstan going round
As the great tides rose and fell.

The sailors' songs, the Captain's shout,
The boatswain's whistle piping shrill,
And the roar as the anchor chain runs out,—
I often hear them still.

I can see them still, the sun on their gear,
The shining streak as the hulls careen,
And the flag at the peak unfurling,—clear
As a picture on a screen.

The fog still hangs on the long tide-rips,
The gulls go wavering to and fro,
But where are all the beautiful ships
I knew so long ago?

The Garden of Dreams

My heart is a garden of dreams
Where you walk when day is done,
Fair as the royal flowers,
Calm as the lingering sun.

Never a drouth comes there,
Nor any frost that mars,
Only the wind of love
Under the early stars,—

The living breath that moves
Whispering to and fro,
Like the voice of God in the dusk

Of the garden long ago.

Garden Magic

Within my stone-walled garden
(I see her standing now,
Uplifted in the twilight,
With glory on her brow!)

I love to walk at evening
And watch, when winds are low,
The new moon in the tree-tops,
Because she loved it so!

And there entranced I listen,
While flowers and winds confer,
And all their conversation
Is redolent of her.

I love the trees that guard it,
Upstanding and serene,
So noble, so undaunted,
Because that was her mien.

I love the brook that bounds it,
Because its silver voice
Is like her bubbling laughter
That made the world rejoice.

I love the golden jonquils,
Because she used to say,
If soul could choose a color
It would be clothed as they.

I love the blue-gray iris,
Because her eyes were blue,
Sea-deep and heaven-tender
In meaning and in hue.

I love the small wild roses,
Because she used to stand
Adoringly above them
And bless them with her hand.

These were her boon companions.
But more than all the rest

I love the April lilac,
Because she loved it best.

Soul of undying rapture!
How love's enchantment clings,
With sorcery and fragrance,
About familiar things!

In Gold Lacquer

Gold are the great trees overhead,
And gold the leaf-strewn grass,
As though a cloth of gold were spread
To let a seraph pass.
And where the pageant should go by,
Meadow and wood and stream,
The world is all of lacquered gold,
Expectant as a dream.

Against the sunset's burning gold,
Etched in dark monotone
Behind its alley of grey trees
And gateposts of grey stone,
Stands the Old Manse, about whose eaves
An air of mystery clings,
Abandoned to the lonely peace
Of bygone ghostly things.

In molten gold the river winds
With languid sweep and turn,
Beside the red-gold wooded hill
Yellowed with ash and fern.
The streets are tiled with gold-green shade
And arched with fretted gold,
Ecstatic aisles that richly thread
This minster grim and old.

The air is flecked with filtered gold,—
The shimmer of romance
Whose ageless glamour still must hold
The world as in a trance,
Pouring o'er every time and place
Light of an amber sea,
The spell of all the gladsome things
That have been or shall be.

Aprilian

When April came with sunshine
And showers and lilac bloom,
My heart with sudden gladness
Was like a fragrant room.

Her eyes were heaven's own azure,
As deep as God's own truth.
Her soul was made of rapture
And mystery and youth.

She knew the sorry burden
Of all the ancient years,
Yet could not dwell with sadness
And memory and tears.

With her there was no shadow
Of failure nor despair,
But only loving joyance.
O Heart, how glad we were!

Garden Shadows

When the dawn winds whisper
To the standing corn,
And the rose of morning
From the dark is born,
All my shadowy garden
Seems to grow aware
Of a fragrant presence,
Half expected there.

In the golden shimmer
Of the burning noon,
When the birds are silent
And the poppies swoon,
Once more I behold her
Smile and turn her face,
With its infinite regard,
Its immortal grace.

When the twilight silvers
Every nodding flower,

And the new moon hallows
The first evening hour,
Is it not her footfall
Down the garden walks,
Where the drowsy blossoms
Slumber on their stalks?

In the starry quiet,
When the soul is free,
And a vernal message
Stirs the lilac tree,
Surely I have felt her
Pass and brush my cheek,
With the eloquence of love
That does not need to speak!

In The Day of Battle

In the day of battle,
In the night of dread,
Let one hymn be lifted,
Let one prayer be said.

Not for pride of conquest,
Not for vengeance wrought,
Nor for peace and safety
With dishonour bought!

Praise for faith in freedom,
Our fighting fathers' stay,
Born of dreams and daring,
Bred above dismay.

Prayer for cloudless vision,
And the valiant hand,
That the right may triumph
To the last demand.

Trees

In the Garden of Eden, planted by God,
There were goodly trees in the springing sod,—

Trees of beauty and height and grace,

To stand in splendor before His face.

Apple and hickory, ash and pear,
Oak and beech and the tulip rare,

The trembling aspen, the noble pine,
The sweeping elm by the river line;

Trees for the birds to build and sing,
And the lilac tree for a joy in spring;

Trees to turn at the frosty call
And carpet the ground for their Lord's footfall;

Trees for fruitage and fire and shade,
Trees for the cunning builder's trade;

Wood for the bow, the spear, and the flail,
The keel and the mast of the daring sail;

He made them of every grain and girth
For the use of man in the Garden of Earth.

Then lest the soul should not lift her eyes
From the gift to the Giver of Paradise,

On the crown of a hill, for all to see,
God planted a scarlet maple tree.

The Givers of Life

I

Who called us forth out of darkness and gave us the gift of life,
Who set our hands to the toiling, our feet in the field of strife?

Darkly they mused, predestined to knowledge of viewless things,
Sowing the seed of wisdom, guarding the living springs.

Little they reckoned privation, hunger or hardship or cold,
If only the life might prosper, and the joy that grows not old.

With sorceries subtler than music, with knowledge older than speech,
Gentle as wind in the wheat-field, strong as the tide on the beach,

Out of their beauty and longing, out of their raptures and tears,

In patience and pride they bore us, to war with the warring years.

II

Who looked on the world before them, and summoned and chose our sires,
Subduing the wayward impulse to the will of their deep desires?

Sovereigns of ultimate issues under the greater laws,
Theirs was the mystic mission of the eternal cause;

Confident, tender, courageous, leaving the low for the higher,
Lifting the feet of the nations out of the dust and the mire;

Luring civilization on to the fair and new,
Given God's bidding to follow, having God's business to do.

III

Who strengthened our souls with courage, and taught us the ways of Earth?
Who gave us our patterns of beauty, our standards of flawless worth?

Mothers, unmilitant, lovely, moulding our manhood then,
Walked in their woman's glory, swaying the might of men.

They schooled us to service and honor, modest and clean and fair,—
The code of their worth of living, taught with the sanction of prayer.

They were our sharers of sorrow, they were our makers of joy,
Lighting the lamp of manhood in the heart of the lonely boy.

Haloed with love and with wonder, in sheltered ways they trod,
Seers of sublime divination, keeping the truce of God.

IV

Who called us from youth and dreaming, and set ambition alight,
And made us fit for the contest,—men, by their tender rite?

Sweethearts above our merit, charming our strength and skill
To be the pride of their loving, to be the means of their will.

If we be the builders of beauty, if we be the masters of art,
Theirs were the gleaming ideals, theirs the uplift of the heart.

Truly they measure the lightness of trappings and ease and fame,

For the teeming desire of their yearning is ever and ever the same:

To crown their lovers with gladness, to clothe their sons with delight,
And see the men of their making lords in the best man's right.

Lavish of joy and labor, broken only by wrong,
These are the guardians of being, spirited, sentient and strong.

Theirs is the starry vision, theirs the inspiriting hope,
Since Night, the brooding enchantress, promised that day should ope.

V

Lo, we have built and invented, reasoned, discovered and planned,
To rear us a palace of splendor, and make us a heaven by hand.

We are shaken with dark misgiving, as kingdoms rise and fall;
But the women who went to found them are never counted at all.

Versed in the soul's traditions, skilled in humanity's lore,
They wait for their crown of rapture, and weep for the sins of war.

And behold they turn from our triumphs, as it was in the first of days,
For a little heaven of ardor and a little heartening of praise.

These are the rulers of kingdoms beyond the domains of state,
Martyrs of all men's folly, over-rulers of fate.

These we will love and honor, these we will serve and defend,
Fulfilling the pride of nature, till nature shall have an end.

VI

This is the code unwritten, this is the creed we hold,
Guarding the little and lonely, gladdening the helpless and old,—

Apart from the brunt of the battle our wondrous women shall bide,
For the sake of a tranquil wisdom and the need of a spirit's guide.

Come they into assembly, or keep they another door,
Our makers of life shall lighten the days as the years of yore.

The lure of their laughter shall lead us, the lilt of their words shall sway.
Though life and death should defeat us, their solace shall be our stay.

Veiled in mysterious beauty, vested in magical grace,

They have walked with angels at twilight and looked upon glory's face.

Life we will give for their safety, care for their fruitful ease,
Though we break at the toiling benches or go down in the smoky seas.

This is the gospel appointed to govern a world of men.
Till love has died, and the echoes have whispered the last Amen.

A Fireside Vision

Once I walked the world enchanted
Through the scented woods of spring,
Hand in hand with Love, in rapture
Just to hear a bluebird sing.

Now the lonely winds of autumn
Moan about my gusty eaves,
As I sit beside the fire
Listening to the flying leaves.

As the dying embers settle
And the twilight falls apace,
Through the gloom I see a vision
Full of ardor, full of grace.

When the Architect of Beauty
Breathed the lyric soul in man,
Lo, the being that he fashioned
Was of such a mould and plan!

Bravely through the deepening shadows
Moves that figure half divine,
With its tenderness of bearing,
With its dignity of line.

Eyes more wonderful than evening
With the new moon on the hill,
Mouth with traces of God's humor
In its corners lurking still.

Ah, she smiles, in recollection;
Lays a hand upon my brow;
Rests this head upon Love's bosom!
Surely it is April now!

A Water Color

There's a picture in my room
Lightens many an hour of gloom,—

Cheers me under fortune's frown
And the drudgery of town.

Many and many a winter day
When my soul sees all things gray,

Here is veritable June,
Heart's content and spirit's boon.

It is scarce a hand-breadth wide,
Not a span from side to side,

Yet it is an open door
Looking back to joy once more,

Where the level marshes lie,
A quiet journey of the eye,

And the unsubstantial blue
Makes the fine illusion true.

So I forth and travel there
In the blessed light and air,

Miles of green tranquillity
Down the river to the sea.

Here the sea-birds roam at will,
And the sea-wind on the hill

Brings the hollow pebbly roar
From the dim and rosy shore,

With the very scent and draft
Of the old sea's mighty craft.

I am standing on the dunes,
By some charm that must be June's,

When the magic of her hand
Lays a sea-spell on the land.

And the old enchantment falls
On the blue-gray orchard walls

And the purple high-top boles,
While the orange orioles

Flame and whistle through the green
Of that paradisal scene.

Strolling idly for an hour
Where the elder is in flower,

I can hear the bob-white call
Down beyond the pasture wall.

Musing in the scented heat,
Where the bayberry is sweet,

I can see the shadows run
Up the cliff-side in the sun.

Or I cross the bridge and reach
The mossers' houses on the beach,

Where the bathers on the sand
Lie sea-freshened and sun-tanned.

Thus I pass the gates of time
And the boundaries of clime,

Change the ugly man-made street
For God's country green and sweet.

Fag of body, irk of mind,
In a moment left behind,

Once more I possess my soul
With the poise and self-control

Beauty gives the free of heart
Through the sorcery of art.

Threnody for a Poet

Not in the ancient abbey,
Nor in the city ground,

Not in the lonely mountains,
Nor in the blue profound,
Lay him to rest when his time is come
And the smiling mortal lips are dumb;

But here in the decent quiet
Under the whispering pines,
Where the dogwood breaks in blossom
And the peaceful sunlight shines,
Where wild birds sing and ferns unfold,
When spring comes back in her green and gold.

And when that mortal likeness
Has been dissolved by fire,
Say not above the ashes,
"Here ends a man's desire."
For every year when the bluebirds sing,
He shall be part of the lyric spring.

Then dreamful-hearted lovers
Shall hear in wind and rain
The cadence of his music,
The rhythm of his refrain,
For he was a blade of the April sod
That bowed and blew with the whisper of God.

Dust of the Street

This cosmic dust beneath our feet
Rising to hurry down the street,

Borne by the wind and blown astray
In its erratic, senseless way,

Is the same stuff as you and I—
With knowledge and desire put by.

Thousands of times since time began
It has been used for making man,

Freighted like us with every sense
Of spirit and intelligence,

To walk the world and know the fine
Large consciousness of things divine.

These wandering atoms in their day
Perhaps have passed this very way,

With eager step and flowerlike face,
With lovely ardor, poise, and grace,

On what delightful errands bent,
Passionate, generous, and intent,—

An angel still, though veiled and gloved,
Made to love us and to be loved.

Friends, when the summons comes for me
To turn my back (reluctantly)

On this delightful play, I claim
Only one thing in friendship's name;

And you will not decline a task
So slight, when it is all I ask:

Scatter my ashes in the street
Where avenue and crossway meet.

I beg you of your charity,
No granite and cement for me,

To needlessly perpetuate
An unimportant name and date.

Others may wish to lay them down
On some fair hillside far from town,

Where slim white birches wave and gleam
Beside a shadowy woodland stream,

Or in luxurious beds of fern,
But I would have my dust return

To the one place it loved the best
In days when it was happiest.

To a Young Lady on Her Birthday

The marching years go by
And brush your garment's hem.

The bandits by and by
Will bid you go with them.

Trust not that caravan!
Old vagabonds are they;
They'll rob you if they can,
And make believe it's play.

Make the old robbers give
Of all the spoils they bear,—
Their truth, to help you live,—
Their joy, to keep you fair.

Ask not for gauds nor gold,
Nor fame that falsely rings;
The foolish world grows old
Caring for all these things.

Make all your sweet demands
For happiness alone,
And the years will fill your hands
With treasures rarely known.

The Gift

I said to Life, "How comes it,
With all this wealth in store,
Of beauty, joy, and knowledge,
Thy cry is still for more?

"Count all the years of striving
To make thy burden less,—
The things designed and fashioned
To gladden thy success!

"The treasures sought and gathered
Thy lightest whim to please,—
The loot of all the ages,
The spoil of all the seas!

"Is there no end of labor,
No limit to thy need?
Must man go bowed forever
In bondage to thy greed?"

With tears of pride and passion

She answered, "God above!
I only wait the asking,
To spend it all for love!"

The Cry of the Hillborn

I am homesick for the mountains—
My heroic mother hills—
And the longing that is on me
No solace ever stills.

I would climb to brooding summits
With their old untarnished dreams,
Cool my heart in forest shadows
To the lull of falling streams;

Hear the innocence of aspens
That babble in the breeze,
And the fragrant sudden showers
That patter on the trees.

I am lonely for my thrushes
In their hermitage withdrawn,
Toning the quiet transports
Of twilight and of dawn.

I need the pure, strong mornings,
When the soul of day is still,
With the touch of frost that kindles
The scarlet on the hill;

Lone trails and winding woodroads
To outlooks wild and high,
And the pale moon waiting sundown
Where ledges cut the sky.

I dream of upland clearings
Where cones of sumac burn,
And gaunt and gray-mossed boulders
Lie deep in beds of fern;

The gray and mottled beeches,
The birches' satin sheen,
The majesty of hemlocks
Crowning the blue ravine.

My eyes dim for the skyline
Where purple peaks aspire,
And the forges of the sunset
Flare up in golden fire.

There crests look down unheeding
And see the great winds blow,
Tossing the huddled tree-tops
In gorges far below;

Where cloud-mists from the warm earth
Roll up about their knees,
And hang their filmy tatters
Like prayers upon the trees.

I cry for night-blue shadows
On plain and hill and dome,—
The spell of old enchantments,
The sorcery of home.

A Mountain Gateway

I know a vale where I would go one day,
When June comes back and all the world once more
Is glad with summer. Deep in shade it lies
A mighty cleft between the bosoming hills,
A cool dim gateway to the mountains' heart.

On either side the wooded slopes come down,
Hemlock and beech and chestnut. Here and there
Through the deep forest laurel spreads and gleams,
Pink-white as Daphne in her loveliness.
Among the sunlit shadows I can see
That still perfection from the world withdrawn,
As if the wood-gods had arrested there
Immortal beauty in her breathless flight.

The road winds in from the broad river-lands,
Luring the happy traveller turn by turn
Up to the lofty mountains of the sky.
And as he marches with uplifted face,
Far overhead against the arching blue
Gray ledges overhang from dizzy heights,
Scarred by a thousand winters and untamed.

And where the road runs in the valley's foot,

Through the dark woods a mountain stream comes down,
Singing and dancing all its youth away
Among the boulders and the shallow runs,
Where sunbeams pierce and mossy tree trunks hang
Drenched all day long with murmuring sound and spray.

There light of heart and footfree, I would go
Up to my home among the lasting hills.
Nearing the day's end, I would leave the road,
Turn to the left and take the steeper trail
That climbs among the hemlocks, and at last
In my own cabin doorway sit me down,
Companioned in that leafy solitude
By the wood ghosts of twilight and of peace,
While evening passes to absolve the day
And leave the tranquil mountains to the stars.

And in that sweet seclusion I should hear,
Among the cool-leafed beeches in the dusk,
The calm-voiced thrushes at their twilight hymn.
So undistraught, so rapturous, so pure,
They well might be, in wisdom and in joy,
The seraphs singing at the birth of time
The unworn ritual of eternal things.

Morning in the Hills

How quiet is the morning in the hills!
The stealthy shadows of the summer clouds
Trail through the cañon, and the mountain stream
Sounds his sonorous music far below
In the deep-wooded wind-enchanted cove.

Hemlock and aspen, chestnut, beech, and fir
Go tiering down from storm-worn crest and ledge,
While in the hollows of the dark ravine
See the red road emerge, then disappear
Towards the wide plain and fertile valley lands.

My forest cabin half-way up the glen
Is solitary, save for one wise thrush,
The sound of falling water, and the wind
Mysteriously conversing with the leaves.

Here I abide unvisited by doubt,
Dreaming of far-off turmoil and despair,

The race of men and love and fleeting time,
What life may be, or beauty, caught and held
For a brief moment at eternal poise.

What impulse now shall quicken and make live
This outward semblance and this inward self?
One breath of being fills the bubble world,
Colored and frail, with fleeting change on change.

Surely some God contrived so fair a thing
In a vast leisure of uncounted days,
And touched it with the breath of living joy,
Wondrous and fair and wise! It must be so.

A Wood-path

At evening and at morning
By an enchanted way
I walk the world in wonder,
And have no word to say.

It is the path we traversed
One twilight, thou and I;
Thy beauty all a rapture,
My spirit all a cry.

The red leaves fall upon it,
The moon and mist and rain,
But not the magic footfall
That made its meaning plain.

Weather of the Soul

There is a world of being
We range from pole to pole,
Through seasons of the spirit
And weather of the soul.

It has its new-born Aprils,
With gladness in the air,
Its golden Junes of rapture,
Its winters of despair.

And in its tranquil autumns
We halt to re-enforce
Our tattered scarlet pennons
With valor and resource.

From undiscovered regions
Only the angels know,
Great winds of aspiration
Perpetually blow,

To free the sap of impulse
From torpor of distrust,
And into flowers of joyance
Quicken the sentient dust.

From nowhere of a sudden
Loom sudden clouds of fault,
With thunders of oppression
And lightnings of revolt.

With hush of apprehension
And quaking of the heart,
There breed the storms of anger,
And floods of sorrow start.

And there shall fall,—how gently!—
To make them fertile yet,
The rain of absolution
On acres of regret.

Till snows of mercy cover
The dream that shall come true,
When time makes all things wondrous,
And life makes all things new.

Here and Now

Where is Heaven? Is it not
Just a friendly garden plot,
Walled with stone and roofed with sun,
Where the days pass one by one,
Not too fast and not too slow,
Looking backward as they go
At the beauties left behind
To transport the pensive mind!

Is it not a greening ground
With a river for its bound,
And a wood-thrush to prolong
Fragrant twilights with his song,
When the peonies in June
Wait the rising of the moon,
And the music of the stream
Voices its immortal dream!

There each morning will renew
The miracle of light and dew,
And the soul may joy to praise
The Lord of roses and of days;
There the caravan of noon
Halts to hear the cricket's tune,
Fifing there for all who pass
The anthem of the summer grass!

Does not Heaven begin that day
When the eager heart can say,
Surely God is in this place,
I have seen Him face to face
In the loveliness of flowers,
In the service of the showers,
And His voice has talked to me
In the sunlit apple tree.

I can feel Him in my heart,
When the tears of knowledge start
For another's joy or woe,
Where the lonely soul must go.
Yea, I learned His very look,
When we walked beside the brook,
And you smiled and touched my hand.
God is love... I understand.

The Angel of Joy

There is no grief for me
Nor sadness any more;
For since I first knew thee
Great Joy has kept my door.

That angel of the calm
All-comprehending smile,
No menace can dismay,

No falsity beguile.

Out of the house of life
Before him fled away
Languor, regret, and strife
And sorrow on that day.

Grim fear, unmanly doubt,
And impotent despair
Went at his bidding forth
Among the things that were,—

Leaving a place all clean,
Resounding of the sea
And decked with forest green,
To be a home for thee.

The Homestead.

Here we came when love was young.
Now that love is old,
Shall we leave the floor unswept
And the hearth acold?

Here the hill-wind in the dusk.
Wandering to and fro,
Moves the moonflowers, like a ghost
Of the long ago.

Here from every doorway looks
A remembered face,
Every sill and panel wears
A familiar grace.

Let the windows smile again
To the morning light,
And the door stand open wide
When the moon is bright.

Let the breeze of twilight blow
Through the silent hall,
And the dreaming rafters hear
How the thrushes call.

Oh, be merciful and fond
To the house that gave

All its best to shelter love,
Built when love was brave!

Here we came when love was young,
Now that love is old,
Never let its day be lone,
Nor its heart acold!

"The Starry Midnight Whispers"

The starry midnight whispers,
As I muse before the fire
On the ashes of ambition
And the embers of desire,

"Life has no other logic,
And time no other creed,
Than: 'I for joy will follow.
Where thou for love dost lead!'"

A Lyric

Oh, once I could not understand
The sob within the throat of spring,—
The shrilling of the frogs, nor why
The birds so passionately sing.

That was before your beauty came
And stooped to teach my soul desire,
When on these mortal lips you laid
The magic and immortal fire.

I wondered why the sea should seem
So gray, so lonely, and so old;
The sigh of level-driving snows
In winter so forlornly cold.

I wondered what it was could give
The scarlet autumn pomps their pride.
And paint with colors not of earth
The glory of the mountainside.

I could not tell why youth should dream
And worship at the evening star,

And yet must go with eager feet
Where danger and where splendor are.

I could not guess why men at times,
Beholding beauty, should go mad
With joy or sorrow or despair
Or some unknown delight they had.

I wondered what they had received
From Time's inexorable hand
So full of loveliness and doom.
But now, ah, now I understand!

"April Now in Morning Clad"

April now in morning clad
Like a gleaming oread,
With the south wind in her voice,
Comes to bid the world rejoice.

With the sunlight on her brow,
Through her veil of silver showers,
April o'er New England now
Trails her robe of woodland flowers,—

Violet and anemone;
While along the misty sea,
Pipe at lip, she seems to blow
Haunting airs of long ago.

Nike

What do men give thanks for?
I give thanks for one,
Lovelier than morning,
Dearer than the sun.

Such a head the victors
Must have praised and known,
With that breast and bearing,
Nike's very own—

As superb, untrammeled,
Rhythmed and poised and free

As the strong pure sea-wind
Walking on the sea;

Such a hand as Beauty
Uses with full heart,
Seeking for her freedom
In new shapes of art;

Soft as rain in April,
Quiet as the days
Of the purple asters
And the autumn haze;

With a soul more subtle
Than the light of stars,
Frailer than a moth's wing
To the touch that mars;

Wise with all the silence
Of the waiting hills,
When the gracious twilight
Wakes in them and thrills;

With a voice more tender
Than the early moon
Hears among the thrushes
In the woods of June;

Delicate as grasses
When they lift and stir—
One sweet lyric woman—
I give thanks for her.

The Enchanted Traveller

We travelled empty-handed
With hearts all fear above,
For we ate the bread of friendship,
We drank the wine of love.

Through many a wondrous autumn,
Through many a magic spring,
We hailed the scarlet banners,
We heard the blue-bird sing.

We looked on life and nature

With the eager eyes of youth,
And all we asked or cared for
Was beauty, joy, and truth.

We found no other wisdom,
We learned no other way,
Than the gladness of the morning,
The glory of the day.

So all our earthly treasure
Shall go with us, my dears,
Aboard the Shadow Liner,
Across the sea of years.

Spring's Saraband

Over the hills of April
With soft winds hand in hand,
Impassionate and dreamy-eyed,
Spring leads her saraband.
Her garments float and gather
And swirl along the plain,
Her headgear is the golden sun,
Her cloak the silver rain.

With color and with music,
With perfumes and with pomp,
By meadowland and upland,
Through pasture, wood, and swamp,
With promise and enchantment
Leading her mystic mime,
She comes to lure the world anew
With joy as old as time.

Quick lifts the marshy chorus
To transport, trill on trill;
There's not a rod of stony ground
Unanswering on the hill.
The brooks and little rivers
Dance down their wild ravines,
And children in the city squares
Keep time, to tambourines.

The bluebird in the orchard
Is lyrical for her,
The blackbird with his meadow pipe

Sets all the wood astir,
The hooded white spring-beauties
Are curtsying in the breeze,
The blue hepaticas are out
Under the chestnut trees.

The maple buds make glamor,
Viburnum waves its bloom,
The daffodils and tulips
Are risen from the tomb.
The lances of Narcissus
Have pierced the wintry mold;
The commonplace seems paradise
Through veils of greening gold.

O heart, hear thou the summons,
Put every grief away,
When all the motley masques of earth
Are glad upon a day.
Alack, that any mortal
Should less than gladness bring
Into the choral joy that sounds
The saraband of spring!

Triumphalis

Soul, art thou sad again
With the old sadness?
Thou shalt be glad again
With a new gladness,
When April sun and rain
Mount to the teeming brain
With the earth madness.

When from the mould again,
Spurning disaster,
Spring shoots unfold again,
Follow thou faster
Out of the drear domain
Of dark, defeat, and pain,
Praising the Master.

Hope for thy guide again,
Ample and splendid;
Love at thy side again,
All doubting ended;

(Ah, by the dragon slain,
For nothing small or vain
Michael contended!)

Thou shalt take heart again,
No more despairing;
Play thy great part again,
Loving and caring.
Hark, how the gold refrain
Runs through the iron strain,
Splendidly daring!

Thou shalt grow strong again,
Confident, tender,—
Battle with wrong again,
Be truth's defender,—
Of the immortal train,
Born to attempt, attain,
Never surrender!

"Now the Lengthening Twilights Hold"

Now the lengthening twilights hold
Tints of lavender and gold,
And the marshy places ring
With the pipers of the spring.

Now the solitary star
Lays a path on meadow streams,
And I know it is not far
To the open door of dreams.

Lord of April, in my hour
May the dogwood be in flower,
And my angel through the dome
Of spring twilight lead me home.

The Soul of April

Over the wintry threshold
Who comes with joy to-day,
So frail, yet so enduring,
To triumph o'er dismay?

Ah, quick her tears are springing,
And quickly they are dried,
For sorrow walks before her,
But gladness walks beside.

She comes with gusts of laughter,—
The music as of rills;
With tenderness and sweetness,—
The wisdom of the hills.

Her hands are strong to comfort,
Her heart is quick to heed.
She knows the signs of sadness,
She knows the voice of need.

There is no living creature,
However poor or small,
But she will know its trouble,
And hasten to its call.

Oh, well they fare forever,
By mighty dreams possessed,
Whose hearts have lain a moment
On that eternal breast.

An April Morning

Once more in misted April
The world is growing green.
Along the winding river
The plumey willows lean.

Beyond the sweeping meadows
The looming mountains rise,
Like battlements of dreamland
Against the brooding skies.

In every wooded valley
The buds are breaking through,
As though the heart of all things
No languor ever knew.

The golden-wings and bluebirds
Call to their heavenly choirs.
The pines are blued and drifted
With smoke of brushwood fires.

And in my sister's garden
Where little breezes run,
The golden daffodillies
Are blowing in the sun.

Earth Voices

I

I heard the spring wind whisper
Above the brushwood fire,
"The world is made forever
Of transport and desire.

I am the breath of being,
The primal urge of things;
I am the whirl of star dust,
I am the lift of wings.

"I am the splendid impulse
That comes before the thought,
The joy and exaltation
Wherein the life is caught.

"Across the sleeping furrows
I call the buried seed,
And blade and bud and blossom
Awaken at my need.

"Within the dying ashes
I blow the sacred spark,
And make the hearts of lovers
To leap against the dark."

II

I heard the spring light whisper
Above the dancing stream,
"The world is made forever
In likeness of a dream.

"I am the law of planets,
I am the guide of man;
The evening and the morning

Are fashioned to my plan.

"I tint the dawn with crimson,
I tinge the sea with blue;
My track is in the desert,
My trail is in the dew.

"I paint the hills with color,
And in my magic dome
I light the star of evening
To steer the traveller home.

"Within the house of being,
I feed the lamp of truth
With tales of ancient wisdom
And prophecies of youth."

III

I heard the spring rain murmur
Above the roadside flower,
"The world is made forever
In melody and power.

"I keep the rhythmic measure
That marks the steps of time,
And all my toil is fashioned
To symmetry and rhyme.

"I plow the untilled upland,
I ripe the seeding grass,
And fill the leafy forest
With music as I pass.

"I hew the raw, rough granite
To loveliness of line,
And when my work is finished,
Behold, it is divine!

"I am the master-builder
In whom the ages trust.
I lift the lost perfection
To blossom from the dust."

IV

Then Earth to them made answer,
As with a slow refrain
Born of the blended voices
Of wind and sun and rain,

"This is the law of being
That links the threefold chain:
The life we give to beauty
Returns to us again."

Resurgam

Lo, now comes the April pageant
And the Easter of the year.
Now the tulip lifts her chalice,
And the hyacinth his spear;
All the daffodils and jonquils
With their hearts of gold are here.
Child of the immortal vision,
What hast thou to do with fear?

When the summons wakes the impulse,
And the blood beats in the vein,
Let no grief thy dream encumber,
No regret thy thought detain.
Through the scented bloom-hung valleys,
Over tillage, wood and plain,
Comes the soothing south wind laden
With the sweet impartial rain.

All along the roofs and pavements
Pass the volleying silver showers,
To unfold the hearts of humans
And the frail unanxious flowers.
Breeding fast in sunlit places,
Teeming life puts forth her powers,
And the migrant wings come northward
On the trail of golden hours.

Over intervale and upland
Sounds the robin's interlude
From his tree-top spire at evening
Where no unbeliefs intrude.
Every follower of beauty
Finds in the spring solitude
Sanctuary and persuasion

Where the mysteries still brood.

Now the bluebird in the orchard,
A warm sighing at the door,
And the soft haze on the hillside,
Lure the houseling to explore
The perennial enchanted
Lovely world and all its lore;
While the early tender twilight
Breathes of those who come no more.

By full brimming river margins
Where the scents of brush fires blow,
Through the faint green mist of springtime,
Dreaming glad-eyed lovers go,
Touched with such immortal madness
Not a thing they care to know
More than those who caught life's secret
Countless centuries ago.

In old Egypt for Osiris,
Putting on the green attire,
With soft hymns and choric dancing
They went forth to greet the fire
Of the vernal sun, whose ardor
His earth children could inspire;
And the ivory flutes would lead them
To the slake of their desire.

In remembrance of Adonis
Did the Dorian maidens sing
Linus songs of joy and sorrow
For the coming back of spring,—
Sorrow for the wintry death
Of each irrevocable thing,
Joy for all the pangs of beauty
The returning year could bring.

Now the priests and holy women
With sweet incense, chant and prayer,
Keep His death and resurrection
Whose new love bade all men share
Immortality of kindness,
Living to make life more fair.
Wakened to such wealth of being,
Who would not arise and dare?

Seeing how each new fulfilment

Issues at the call of need
From infinitudes of purpose
In the core of soul and seed,
Who shall set the bounds of puissance
Or the formulas of creed?
Truth awaits the test of beauty,
Good is proven in the deed.

Therefore, give thy spring renascence,—
Freshened ardor, dreams and mirth,—
To make perfect and replenish
All the sorry fault and dearth
Of the life from whose enrichment
Thine aspiring will had birth;
Take thy part in the redemption
Of thy kind from bonds of earth.

So shalt thou, absorbed in beauty,
Even in this mortal clime
Share the life that is eternal,
Brother to the lords of time,—
Virgil, Raphael, Gautama,—
Builders of the world sublime.
Yesterday was not earth's evening
Every morning is our prime.

All that can be worth the rescue
From oblivion and decay,—
Joy and loveliness and wisdom,—
In thyself, without dismay
Thou shalt save and make enduring
Through each word and act, to sway
The hereafter to a likeness
Of thyself in other clay.

Still remains the peradventure,
Soul pursues an orbit here
Like those unreturning comets,
Sweeping on a vast career,
By an infinite directrix,
Focussed to a finite sphere,—
Nurtured in an earthly April,
In what realm to reappear?

Easter Eve

If I should tell you I saw Pan lately down by the shallows of Silvermine,
Blowing an air on his pipe of willow, just as the moon began to shine;
Or say that, coming from town on Wednesday, I met Christ walking in Ponus Street;
You might remark, "Our friend is flighty! Visions, for want of enough red meat!"

Then let me ask you. Last December, when there was skating on Wampanaw,
Among the weeds and sticks and grasses under the hard black ice I saw
An old mud-turtle poking about, as if he were putting his house to rights,
Stiff with the cold perhaps, yet knowing enough to prepare for the winter nights.

And here he is on a log this morning, sunning himself as calm as you please.
But I want to know, when the lock of winter was sprung of a sudden, who kept the keys?
Who told old nibbler to go to sleep safe and sound with the lily roots,
And then in the first warm days of April—out to the sun with the greening shoots?

By night a flock of geese went over, honking north on the trails of air,
The spring express—but who despatched it, equipped with speed and cunning care?
Hark to our bluebird down in the orchard trolling his chant of the happy heart,
As full of light as a theme of Mozart's—but where did he learn that more than art?

Where the river winds through grassy meadows, as sure as the south wind brings the rain,
Sounding his reedy note in the alders, the redwing comes back to his nest again.
Are these not miracles? Prompt you answer: "Merely the prose of natural fact;
Nothing but instinct plain and patent, born in the creatures, that bids them act."

Well, I have an instinct as fine and valid, surely, as that of the beasts and birds,
Concerning death and the life immortal, too deep for logic, too vague for words.
No trace of beauty can pass or perish, but other beauty is somewhere born;
No seed of truth or good be planted, but the yield must grow as the growing corn.

Therefore this ardent mind and spirit I give to the glowing days of earth.
To be wrought by the Lord of life to something of lasting import and lovely worth.
If the toil I give be without self-seeking, bestowed to the limit of will and power,
To fashion after some form ideal the instant task and the waiting hour,

It matters not though defeat undo me, though faults betray me and sorrows scar,
Already I share the life eternal with the April buds and the evening star.
The slim new moon is my sister now; the rain, my brother; the wind, my friend.
Is it not well with these forever? Can the soul of man fare ill in the end?

Now is the Time of Year

Now is the time of year
When all the flutes begin,—
The redwing bold and clear,
The rainbird far and thin.

In all the waking lands
There's not a wilding thing
But knows and understands
The burden of the spring.

Now every voice alive
By rocky wood and stream
Is lifted to revive
The ecstasy, the dream.

For Nature, never old,
But busy as of yore,
From sun and rain and mould
Is making spring once more.

She sounds her magic note
By river-marge and hill,
And every woodland throat
Re-echoes with a thrill.

O mother of our days,
Hearing thy music call.
Teach us to know thy ways
And fear no more at all!

The Redwing

I hear you, Brother, I hear you,
Down in the alder swamp,
Springing your woodland whistle
To herald the April pomp!

First of the moving vanguard,
In front of the spring you come,
Where flooded waters sparkle
And streams in the twilight hum.

You sound the note of the chorus
By meadow and woodland pond,
Till, one after one up-piping,
A myriad throats respond.

I see you, Brother, I see you,
With scarlet under your wing,
Flash through the ruddy maples,

Leading the pageant of spring.

Earth has put off her raiment
Wintry and worn and old,
For the robe of a fair young sibyl.
Dancing in green and gold.

I heed you, Brother. To-morrow
I, too, in the great employ,
Will shed my old coat of sorrow
For a brand-new garment of joy.

The Rainbird

I hear a rainbird singing
Far off. How fine and clear
His plaintive voice comes ringing
With rapture to the ear!

Over the misty wood-lots,
Across the first spring heat,
Comes the enchanted cadence,
So clear, so solemn-sweet.

How often I have hearkened
To that high pealing strain
Across wild cedar barrens,
Under the soft gray rain!

How often I have wondered,
And longed in vain to know
The source of that enchantment,
That touch of human woe!

O brother, who first taught thee
To haunt the teeming spring
With that sad mortal wisdom
Which only age can bring?

Lament

When you hear the white-throat pealing
From a tree-top far away,
And the hills are touched with purple

At the borders of the day;

When the redwing sounds his whistle
At the coming on of spring,
And the joyous April pipers
Make the alder marshes ring;

When the wild new breath of being
Whispers to the world once more,
And before the shrine of beauty
Every spirit must adore;

When long thoughts come back with twilight,
And a tender deepened mood
Shows the eyes of the beloved
Like the hepaticas in the wood;

Ah, remember, when to nothing
Save to love your heart gives heed,
And spring takes you to her bosom,—
So it was with Golden Weed!

Under the April Moon

Oh, well the world is dreaming
Under the April moon,
Her soul in love with beauty,
Her senses all a-swoon!

Pure hangs the silver crescent
Above the twilight wood,
And pure the silver music
Wakes from the marshy flood.

O Earth, with all thy transport,
How comes it life should seem
A shadow in the moonlight,
A murmur in a dream?

The Flute of Spring

I know a shining meadow stream
That winds beneath an Eastern hill,
And all year long in sun or gloom

Its murmuring voice is never still.

The summer dies more gently there,
The April flowers are earlier,—
The first warm rain-wind from the Sound
Sets all their eager hearts astir.

And there when lengthening twilights fall
As softly as a wild bird's wing,
Across the valley in the dusk
I hear the silver flute of spring.

Spring Night

In the wondrous star-sown night,
In the first sweet warmth of spring,
I lie awake and listen
To hear the glad earth sing.

I hear the brook in the wood
Murmuring, as it goes,
The song of the happy journey
Only the wise heart knows.

I hear the trilling note
Of the tree-frog under the hill,
And the clear and watery treble
Of his brother, silvery shrill.

And then I wander away
Through the mighty forest of Sleep,
To follow the fairy music
To the shore of an endless deep.

Bloodroot

When April winds arrive
And the soft rains are here,
Some morning by the roadside
These Fairy folk appear.

We never see their coming,
However sharp our eyes;
Each year as if by magic

They take us by surprise.

Along the ragged woodside
And by the green spring-run,
Their small white heads are nodding
And twinkling in the sun.

They crowd across the meadow
In innocence and mirth,
As if there were no sorrow
In all this wondrous earth.

So frail, so unregarded,
And yet about them clings
A sorcery of welcome,—
The joy of common things.

Perhaps their trail of beauty
Across the pasture sod
In jubilant procession
Is where an angel trod.

Daffodil's Return

What matter if the sun be lost?
What matter though the sky be gray?
There's joy enough about the house,
For Daffodil comes home to-day.

There's news of swallows on the air,
There's word of April on the way,
They're calling flowers within the street,
And Daffodil comes home to-day.

O who would care what fate may bring,
Or what the years may take away!
There's life enough within the hour,
For Daffodil comes home to-day.

Now the Lilac Tree's in Bud

Now the lilac tree's in bud,
And the morning birds are loud.
Now a stirring in the blood

Moves the heart of every crowd.

Word has gone abroad somewhere
Of a great impending change.
There's a message in the air
Of an import glad and strange.

Not an idler in the street,
But is better off to-day.
Not a traveller you meet,
But has something wise to say.

Now there's not a road too long,
Not a day that is not good,
Not a mile but hears a song
Lifted from the misty wood.

Down along the Silvermine
That's the blackbird's cheerful note!
You can see him flash and shine
With the scarlet on his coat.

Now the winds are soft with rain,
And the twilight has a spell,
Who from gladness could refrain
Or with olden sorrows dwell?

White Iris

White Iris was a princess
In a kingdom long ago,
Mysterious as moonlight
And silent as the snow.

She drew the world in wonder
And swayed it with desire,
Ere Babylon was builded
Or a stone laid in Tyre.

Yet here within my garden
Her loveliness appears,
Undimmed by any sorrow
Of all the tragic years.

How kind that earth should treasure
So beautiful a thing—

All mystical enchantment,
To stir our hearts in spring!

The Tree of Heaven

Young foreign-born Ailanthus,
Because he grew so fast,
We scorned his easy daring
And doubted it would last.

But lo, when autumn gathers
And all the woods are old,
He stands in green and salmon,
A glory to behold!

Among the ancient monarchs
His airy tent is spread.
His robe of coronation
Is tasseled rosy red.

With something strange and Eastern,
His height and grace proclaim
His lineage and title
Is that celestial name.

This is the Tree of Heaven,
Which seems to say to us,
"Behold how rife is beauty,
And how victorious!"

Peony

"Pionia virtutem habet occultam."
Arnoldus Villanova—1235-1313.

Arnoldus Villanova
Six hundred years ago
Said Peonies have magic,
And I believe it so.
There stands his learned dictum
Which any boy may read,
But he who learns the secret
Will be made wise indeed.

Astrologer and doctor
In the science of his day,
Have we so far outstripped him?
What more is there to say?
His medieval Latin
Records the truth for us,
Which I translate—virtutem
Habet occultam—thus:

She hath a deep-hid virtue
No other flower hath.
When summer comes rejoicing
A-down my garden path,
In opulence of color,
In robe of satin sheen,
She casts o'er all the hours
Her sorcery serene.

A subtile, heartening fragrance
Comes piercing the warm hush,
And from the greening woodland
I hear the first wild thrush.
They move my heart to pity
For all the vanished years,
With ecstasy of longing
And tenderness of tears.

By many names we call her,—
Pale exquisite Aurore,
Luxuriant Gismonda
Or sunny Couronne D'Or.
What matter,—Grandiflora,
A queen in some proud book,
Or sweet familiar Piny
With her old-fashioned look?

The crowding Apple blossoms
Above the orchard wall;
The Moonflower in August
When eerie nights befall;
Chrysanthemum in autumn,
Whose pageantries appear
With mystery and silence
To deck the dying year;

And many a mystic flower
Of the wildwood I have known,
But Pionia Arnoldi

Hath a transport all her own.
For Peony, my Peony,
Hath strength to make me whole,—
She gives her heart of beauty
For the healing of my soul.

Arnoldus Villanova,
Though earth is growing old,
As long as life has longing
Your guess at truth will hold.
Still works the hidden power
After a thousand springs,—
The medicine for heartache
That lurks in lovely things.

The Urban Pan

Once more the magic days are come
With stronger sun and milder air;
The shops are full of daffodils;
There's golden leisure everywhere.
I heard my Lou this morning shout:
"Here comes the hurdy-gurdy man!"
And through the open window caught
The piping of the urban Pan.

I laid my wintry task aside,
And took a day to follow joy:
The trail of beauty and the call
That lured me when I was a boy.
I looked, and there looked up at me
A smiling, swarthy, hairy man
With kindling eye—and well I knew
The piping of the urban Pan.

He caught my mood; his hat was off;
I tossed the ungrudged silver down.
The cunning vagrant, every year
He casts his spell upon the town!
And we must fling him, old and young,
Our dimes or coppers, as we can;
And every heart must leap to hear
The piping of the urban Pan.

The music swells and fades again,
And I in dreams am far away,

Where a bright river sparkles down
To meet a blue Aegean bay.
There, in the springtime of the world,
Are dancing fauns, and in their van,
Is one who pipes a deathless tune—
The earth-born and the urban Pan.

And so he follows down the block,
A troop of children in his train,
The light-foot dancers of the street
Enamored of the reedy strain.
I hear their laughter rise and ring
Above the noise of truck and van,
As down the mellow wind fades out
The piping of the urban Pan.

The Sailing of the Fleets

Now the spring is in the town,
Now the wind is in the tree,
And the wintered keels go down
To the calling of the sea.

Out from mooring, dock, and slip,
Through the harbor buoys they glide,
Drawing seaward till they dip
To the swirling of the tide.

One by one and two by two,
Down the channel turns they go,
Steering for the open blue
Where the salty great airs blow;

Craft of many a build and trim,
Every stitch of sail unfurled,
Till they hang upon the rim
Of the azure ocean world.

Who has ever, man or boy,
Seen the sea all flecked with gold,
And not longed to go with joy
Forth upon adventures bold?

Who could bear to stay indoor,
Now the wind is in the street,
For the creaking of the oar

And the tugging of the sheet!

Now the spring is in the town,
Who would not a rover be,
When the wintered keels go down
To the calling of the sea?

'Tis May Now in New England

'Tis May now in New England
And through the open door
I see the creamy breakers,
I hear the hollow roar.

Back to the golden marshes
Comes summer at full tide,
But not the golden comrade
Who was the summer's pride.

In Early May

O my dear, the world to-day
Is more lovely than a dream!
Magic hints from far away
Haunt the woodland, and the stream
Murmurs in his rocky bed
Things that never can be said.

Starry dogwood is in flower,
Gleaming through the mystic woods.
It is beauty's perfect hour
In the wild spring solitudes.
Now the orchards in full blow
Shed their petals white as snow.

All the air is honey-sweet
With the lilacs white and red,
Where the blossoming branches meet
In an arbor overhead.
And the laden cherry trees
Murmur with the hum of bees.

All the earth is fairy green,
And the sunlight filmy gold,

Full of ecstasies unseen,
Full of mysteries untold.
Who would not be out-of-door,
Now the spring is here once more!

Fireflies

The fireflies across the dusk
Are flashing signals through the gloom—
Courageous messengers of light
That dare immensities of doom.

About the seeding meadow-grass,
Like busy watchmen in the street,
They come and go, they turn and pass,
Lighting the way for Beauty's feet.

Or up they float on viewless wings
To twinkle high among the trees,
And rival with soft glimmerings
The shining of the Pleiades.

The stars that wheel above the hill
Are not more wonderful to see,
Nor the great tasks that they fulfill
More needed in eternity.

The Path to Sankoty

It winds along the headlands
Above the open sea—
The lonely moorland footpath
That leads to Sankoty.

The crooning sea spreads sailless
And gray to the world's rim,
Where hang the reeking fog-banks
Primordial and dim.

There fret the ceaseless currents,
And the eternal tide
Chafes over hidden shallows
Where the white horses ride.

The wistful fragrant moorlands
Whose smile bids panic cease,
Lie treeless and cloud-shadowed
In grave and lonely peace.

Across their flowering bosom,
From the far end of day
Blow clean the great soft moor-winds
All sweet with rose and bay.

A world as large and simple
As first emerged for man,
Cleared for the human drama,
Before the play began.

O well the soul must treasure
The calm that sets it free—
The vast and tender skyline,
The sea-turn's wizardry,

Solace of swaying grasses,
The friendship of sweet-fern—
And in the world's confusion
Remembering, must yearn

To tread the moorland footpath
That leads to Sankoty,
Hearing the field-larks shrilling
Beside the sailless sea.

Off Monomoy

Have you sailed Nantucket Sound
By lightship, buoy, and bell,
And lain becalmed at noon
On an oily summer swell?

Lazily drooped the sail,
Moveless the pennant hung,
Sagging over the rail
Idle the main boom swung;

The sea, one mirror of shine
A single breath would destroy,
Save for the far low line

Of treacherous Monomoy.

Yet eastward there toward Spain,
What castled cities rise
From the Atlantic plain,
To our enchanted eyes!

Turret and spire and roof
Looming out of the sea,
Where the prosy chart gives proof
No cape nor isle can be!

Can a vision shine so clear
Wherein no substance dwells?
One almost harks to hear
The sound of the city's bells.

And yet no pealing notes
Within those belfries be,
Save echoes from the throats
Of ship-bells lost at sea.

For none shall anchor there
Save those who long of yore,
When tide and wind were fair,
Sailed and came back no more.

And none shall climb the stairs
Within those ghostly towers,
Save those for whom sad prayers
Went up through fateful hours.

O image of the world,
O mirage of the sea,
Cloud-built and foam-impearled.
What sorcery fashioned thee?

What architect of dream,
What painter of desire,
Conceived that fairy scheme
Touched with fantastic fire?

Even so our city of hope
We mortal dreamers rear
Upon the perilous slope
Above the deep of fear;

Leaving half-known the good

Our kindly earth bestows,
For the feigned beatitude
Of a future no man knows.

Lord of the summer sea,
Whose tides are in thy hand,
Into immensity
The vision at thy command

Fades now, and leaves no sign,—
No light nor bell nor buoy,—
Only the faint low line
Of dangerous Monomoy.

In St. Germain Street

Through the street of St. Germain
March the tattered hosts of rain,

While the wind with vagrant fife
Whips their chilly ranks to life.

From the window I can see
Their ghostly banners blowing free,

As they pass to where the ships
Crowd about the wharves and slips.

There at day's end they embark
To invade the realms of dark,

And the sun comes out again
In the street of St. Germain.

Pan in the Catskills

They say that he is dead, and now no more
The reedy syrinx sounds among the hills,
When the long summer heat is on the land.
But I have heard the Catskill thrushes sing,
And therefore am incredulous of death,
Of pain and sorrow and mortality.

In these blue cañons, deep with hemlock shade,

In solitudes of twilight or of dawn,
I have been rapt away from time and care
By the enchantment of a golden strain
As pure as ever pierced the Thracian wild,
Filling the listener with a mute surmise.

At evening and at morning I have gone
Down the cool trail between the beech-tree boles,
And heard the haunting music of the wood
Ring through the silence of the dark ravine,
Flooding the earth with beauty and with joy
And all the ardors of creation old.

And then within my pagan heart awoke
Remembrance of far-off and fabled years
In the untarnished sunrise of the world,
When clear-eyed Hellas in her rapture heard
A slow mysterious piping wild and keen
Thrill through her vales, and whispered, "It is Pan!"

A New England June

These things I remember
Of New England June,
Like a vivid day-dream
In the azure noon,
While one haunting figure
Strays through every scene,
Like the soul of beauty
Through her lost demesne.

Gardens full of roses
And peonies a-blow
In the dewy morning,
Row on stately row,
Spreading their gay patterns,
Crimson, pied and cream,
Like some gorgeous fresco
Or an Eastern dream.

Nets of waving sunlight
Falling through the trees;
Fields of gold-white daisies
Rippling in the breeze;
Lazy lifting groundswells,
Breaking green as jade

On the lilac beaches,
Where the shore-birds wade.

Orchards full of blossom,
Where the bob-white calls
And the honeysuckle
Climbs the old gray walls;
Groves of silver birches,
Beds of roadside fern,
In the stone-fenced pasture
At the river's turn.

Out of every picture
Still she comes to me
With the morning freshness
Of the summer sea,—
A glory in her bearing,
A sea-light in her eyes,
As if she could not forget
The spell of Paradise.

Thrushes in the deep woods,
With their golden themes,
Fluting like the choirs
At the birth of dreams.
Fireflies in the meadows
At the gate of Night,
With their fairy lanterns
Twinkling soft and bright.

Ah, not in the roses,
Nor the azure noon,
Nor the thrushes' music,
Lies the soul of June.
It is something finer,
More unfading far,
Than the primrose evening
And the silver star;

Something of the rapture
My beloved had,
When she made the morning
Radiant and glad,—
Something of her gracious
Ecstasy of mien,
That still haunts the twilight,
Loving though unseen.

When the ghostly moonlight
Walks my garden ground,
Like a leisurely patrol
On his nightly round,
These things I remember
Of the long ago,
While the slumbrous roses
Neither care nor know.

The Tent of Noon

Behold, now, where the pageant of high June
Halts in the glowing noon!
The trailing shadows rest on plain and hill;
The bannered hosts are still,
While over forest crown and mountain head
The azure tent is spread.

The song is hushed in every woodland throat;
Moveless the lilies float;
Even the ancient ever-murmuring sea
Sighs only fitfully;
The cattle drowse in the field-corner's shade;
Peace on the world is laid.

It is the hour when Nature's caravan,
That bears the pilgrim Man
Across the desert of uncharted time
To his far hope sublime,
Rests in the green oasis of the year,
As if the end drew near.

Ah, traveller, hast thou naught of thanks or praise
For these fleet halcyon days?—
No courage to uplift thee from despair
Born with the breath of prayer?
Then turn thee to the lilied field once more!
God stands in his tent door.

Children of Dream

The black ash grows in the swampy ground,
The white ash in the dry;
The thrush he holds to the woodland bound,

The hawk to the open sky.

The trout he runs to the mountain brook,
The swordfish keeps the sea;
The brown bear knows where the blueberry grows.
The clover calls the bee.

The locust sings in the August noon,
The frog in the April night;
The iris loves the meadow-land,
The laurel loves the height.

And each will hold his tenure old
Of earth and sun and stream,
For all are creatures of desire
And children of a dream.

Roadside Flowers

We are the roadside flowers,
Straying from garden grounds,—
Lovers of idle hours,
Breakers of ordered bounds.

If only the earth will feed us,
If only the wind be kind,
We blossom for those who need us,
The stragglers left behind.

And lo, the Lord of the Garden,
He makes his sun to rise,
And his rain to fall with pardon
On our dusty paradise.

On us he has laid the duty,—
The task of the wandering breed,—
To better the world with beauty,
Wherever the way may lead.

Who shall inquire of the season,
Or question the wind where it blows?
We blossom and ask no reason.
The Lord of the Garden knows.

The Garden of Saint Rose

This is a holy refuge,
The garden of Saint Rose,
A fragrant altar to that peace
The world no longer knows.

Below a solemn hillside,
Within the folding shade
Of overhanging beech and pine
Its walls and walks are laid.

Cool through the heat of summer,
Still as a sacred grove,
It has the rapt unworldly air
Of mystery and love.

All day before its outlook
The mist-blue mountains loom,
And in its trees at tranquil dusk
The early stars will bloom.

Down its enchanted borders
Glad ranks of color stand,
Like hosts of silent seraphim
Awaiting love's command.

Lovely in adoration
They wait in patient line,
Snow-white and purple and deep gold
About the rose-gold shrine.

And there they guard the silence,
While still from her recess
Through sun and shade Saint Rose looks down
In mellow loveliness.

She seems to say, "O stranger,
Behold how loving care
That gives its life for beauty's sake,
Makes everything more fair!

"Then praise the Lord of gardens
For tree and flower and vine,
And bless all gardeners who have wrought
A resting place like mine!"

The World Voice

I heard the summer sea
Murmuring to the shore
Some endless story of a wrong
The whole world must deplore.

I heard the mountain wind
Conversing with the trees
Of an old sorrow of the hills,
Mysterious as the sea's.

And all that haunted day
It seemed that I could hear
The echo of an ancient speech
Ring in my listening ear.

And then it came to me,
That all that I had heard
Was my own heart in the sea's voice
And the wind's lonely word.

Songs of the Grass

I

ON THE DUNES

Here all night on the dunes
In the rocking wind we sleep,
Watched by sentry stars,
Lulled by the drone of the deep.

Till hark, in the chill of the dawn
A field lark wakes and cries,
And over the floor of the sea
We watch the round sun rise.

The world is washed once more
In a tide of purple and gold,
And the heart of the land is filled
With desires and dreams untold.

II

LORD OF MORNING

Lord of morning, light of day,
Sacred color-kindling sun,
We salute thee in the way,—
Pilgrims robed in rose and dun.

For thou art a pilgrim too,
Overlord of all our band.
In thy fervor we renew
Quests we do not understand.

At thy summons we arise,
At thy touch put glory on.
And with glad unanxious eyes
Take the journey thou hast gone.

III

THE TRAVELLER

Before the night-blue fades
And the stars are quite gone,
I lift my head
At the noiseless tread
Of the angel of dawn.

I hear no word, yet my heart
Is beating apace;
Then in glory all still
On the eastern hill
I behold his face.

All day through the world he goes,
Making glad, setting free;
Then his day's work done,
On the galleon sun
He sinks in the sea.

The Choristers

When earth was finished and fashioned well,
There was never a musical note to tell
How glad God was, save the voice of the rain

And the sea and the wind on the lonely plain
And the rivers among the hills.
And so God made the marvellous birds
For a choir of joy transcending words,
That the world might hear and comprehend
How rhythm and harmony can mend
The spirits' hurts and ills.

He filled their tiny bodies with fire,
He taught them love for their chief desire,
And gave them the magic of wings to be
His celebrants over land and sea,
Wherever man might dwell.
And to each he apportioned a fragment of song—
Those broken melodies that belong
To the seraphs' chorus, that we might learn
The healing of gladness and discern
In beauty how all is well.

So music dwells in the glorious throats
Forever, and the enchanted notes
Fall with rapture upon our ears,
Moving our hearts to joy and tears
For things we cannot say.
In the wilds the whitethroat sings in the rain
His pure, serene, half-wistful strain;
And when twilight falls the sleeping hills
Ring with the cry of the whippoorwills
In the blue dusk far away.

In the great white heart of the winter storm
The chickadee sings, for his heart is warm,
And his note is brave to rally the soul
From doubt and panic to self-control
And elation that knows no fear.
The bluebird comes with the winds of March,
Like a shred of sky on the naked larch;
The redwing follows the April rain
To whistle contentment back again
With his sturdy call of cheer.

The orioles revel through orchard boughs
In their coats of gold for spring's carouse;
In shadowy pastures the bobwhites call,
And the flute of the thrush has a melting fall
Under the evening star.
On the verge of June when peonies blow
And joy comes back to the world we know,

The bobolinks fill the fields of light
With a tangle of music silver-bright
To tell how glad they are.

The tiny warblers fill summer trees
With their exquisite lesser litanies;
The tanager in his scarlet coat
In the hemlock pours from a vibrant throat
His canticle of the sun.
The loon on the lake, the hawk in the sky,
And the sea-gull—each has a piercing cry,
Like outposts set in the lonely vast
To cry "all's well" as Time goes past
And another hour is gone.

But of all the music in God's plan
Of a mystical symphony for man,
I shall remember best of all—
Whatever hereafter may befall
Or pass and cease to be—
The hermit's hymn in the solitudes
Of twilight through the mountain woods,
And the field-larks crying about our doors
On the soft sweet wind across the moors
At morning by the sea.

The Weed's Counsel

Said a traveller by the way
Pausing, "What hast thou to say,
Flower by the dusty road,
That would ease a mortal's load?"

Traveller, hearken unto me!
I will tell thee how to see
Beauties in the earth and sky
Hidden from the careless eye.
I will tell thee how to hear
Nature's music wild and clear,—
Songs of midday and of dark
Such as many never mark,
Lyrics of creation sung
Ever since the world was young.

And thereafter thou shalt know
Neither weariness nor woe.

Thou shalt see the dawn unfold
Artistries of rose and gold,
And the sunbeams on the sea
Dancing with the wind for glee.
The red lilies of the moors
Shall be torches on the floors,
Where the field-lark lifts his cry
To rejoice the passer-by,
In a wide world rimmed with blue
Lovely as when time was new.

And thereafter thou shalt fare
Light of foot and free from care.

I will teach thee how to find
Lost enchantments of the mind
All about thee, never guessed
By indifferent unrest.
Thy distracted thought shall learn
Patience from the roadside fern,
And a sweet philosophy
From the flowering locust tree,—
While thy heart shall not disdain
The consolation of the rain.

Not an acre but shall give
Of its strength to help thee live.

With the many-wintered sun
Shall thy hardy course be run.
And the bright new moon shall be
A lamp to thy felicity.
When green-mantled spring shall come
Past thy door with flute and drum,
And when over wood and swamp
Autumn trails her scarlet pomp,
No misgiving shalt thou know,
Passing glad to rise and go.

So thy days shall be unrolled
Like a wondrous cloth of gold.

When gray twilight with her star
Makes a heaven that is not far,
Touched with shadows and with dreams,
Thou shalt hear the woodland streams
Singing through the starry night

Holy anthems of delight.
So the ecstasy of earth
Shall refresh thee as at birth,
And thou shalt arise each morn
Radiant with a soul reborn.

And this wisdom of a day
None shall ever take away.

What the secret, what the clew
The wayfarer must pursue?
Only one thing he must have
Who would share these transports brave.
Love within his heart must dwell
Like a bubbling roadside well,
For a spring to quicken thought,
Else my counsel comes to naught.
For without that quickening trust
We are less than roadside dust.

This, O traveller, is my creed,—
All the wisdom of the weed!

Then the traveller set his pack
Once more on his dusty back,
And trudged on for many a mile
Fronting fortune with a smile.

The Blue Heron

I see the great blue heron
Rising among the reeds
And floating down the wind,
Like a gliding sail
With the set of the stream.

I hear the two-horse mower
Clacking among the hay,
In the heat of a July noon,
And the driver's voice
As he turns his team.

I see the meadow lilies
Flecked with their darker tan,
The elms, and the great white clouds;
And all the world

Is a passing dream.

Woodland Rain

Shining, shining children
Of the summer rain,
Racing down the valley,
Sweeping o'er the plain!

Rushing through the forest,
Pelting on the leaves,
Drenching down the meadow
With its standing sheaves;

Robed in royal silver,
Girt with jewels gay,
With a gust of gladness
You pass upon your way.

Fresh, ah, fresh behind you,
Sunlit and impearled,
As it was in Eden,
Lies the lovely world!

Summer Storm

The hilltop trees are bowing
Under the coming of storm.
The low, gray clouds are trailing
Like squadrons that sweep and form,
With their ammunition of rain.

Then the trumpeter wind gives signal
To unlimber the viewless guns;
The cattle huddle together;
Indoors the farmer runs;
And the first shot lashes the pane.

They charge through the quiet orchard;
One pear tree is snapped like a wand;
As they sweep from the shattered hillside,
Ruffling the blackened pond,
Ere the sun takes the field again.

Dance of the Sunbeams

When morning is high o'er the hilltops,
On river and stream and lake,
Wherever a young breeze whispers,
The sun-clad dancers wake.

One after one up-springing,
They flash from their dim retreat.
Merry as running laughter
Is the news of their twinkling feet.

Over the floors of azure
Wherever the wind-flaws run,
Sparkling, leaping, and racing,
Their antics scatter the sun.

As long as water ripples
And weather is clear and glad,
Day after day they are dancing,
Never a moment sad.

But when through the field of heaven
The wings of storm take flight,
At a touch of the flying shadows
They falter and slip from sight.

Until at the gray day's ending,
As the squadrons of cloud retire,
They pass in the triumph of sunset
With banners of crimson fire.

The Campfire of the Sun

Lo, now, the journeying sun,
Another day's march done,
Kindles his campfire at the edge of night!
And in the twilight pale
Above his crimson trail,
The stars move out their cordons still and bright.

Now in the darkening hush
A solitary thrush
Sings on in silvery rapture to the deep;

While brooding on her best,
The wandering soul has rest,
And earth receives her sacred gift of sleep.

Summer Streams

All day long beneath the sun
Shining through the fields they run,

Singing in a cadence known
To the seraphs round the throne.

And the traveller drawing near
Through the meadow, halts to hear

Anthems of a natural joy
No disaster can destroy.

All night long from set of sun
Through the starry woods they run,

Singing through the purple dark
Songs to make a traveller hark.

All night long, when winds are low,
Underneath my window go

The immortal happy streams,
Making music through my dreams.

The God of the Wood

Here all the forces of the wood
As one converge,
To make the soul of solitude
Where all things merge.

The sun, the rain-wind, and the rain,
The visiting moon,
The hurrying cloud by peak and plain,
Each with its boon.

Here power attains perfection still
In mighty ease,

That the great earth may have her will
Of joy and peace.

And so through me, the mortal born
Of plasmic clay,
Immortal powers, kind, fierce, forlorn,
And glad, have sway.

Eternal passions, ardors fine,
And monstrous fears,
Rule and rebel, serene, malign,
Or loosed in tears;

Until at last they shall evolve
From griefs and joys
Some steady light, some firm resolve,
Some Godlike poise.

At Sunrise

Now the stars have faded
In the purple chill,
Lo, the sun is kindling
On the eastern hill.

Tree by tree the forest
Takes the golden tinge,
As the shafts of glory
Pierce the summit's fringe.

Rock by rock the ledges
Take the rosy sheen,
As the tide of splendor
Floods the dark ravine.

Like a shining angel
At my cabin door,
Shod with hope and silence,
Day is come once more.

Then, as if in sorrow
That you are not here,
All his magic beauties
Gray and disappear.

At Twilight

Now the fire is lighted
On the chimney stone,
Day goes down the valley,
I am left alone.

Now the misty purple
Floods the darkened vale,
And the stars come out
On the twilight trail.

The mountain river murmurs
In his rocky bed,
And the stealthy shadows
Fill the house with dread.

Then I hear your laughter
At the open door,—
Brightly burns the fire,
I need fear no more.

Moonrise

At the end of the road through the wood
I see the great moon rise.
The fields are flooded with shine,
And my soul with surmise.

What if that mystic orb
With her shadowy beams,
Should be the revealer at last
Of my darkest dreams!

What if this tender fire
In my heart's deep hold
Should be wiser than all the lore
Of the sages of old!

The Queen of Night

Mortal, mortal, have you seen
In the scented summer night,

Great Astarte, clad in green
With a veil of mystic light,
Passing on her silent way,
Pale and lovelier than day?

Mortal, mortal, have you heard,
On an odorous summer eve,
Rumors of an unknown word
Bidding sorrow not to grieve,—
Echoes of a silver voice
Bidding every heart rejoice?

Mortal, when the slim new moon
Hangs above the western hill,
When the year comes round to June
And the leafy world is still,
Then, enraptured, you shall hear
Secrets for a poet's ear.

Mortal, mortal, come with me,
When the moon is rising large,
Through the wood or from the sea,
Or by some lone river marge.
There, entranced, you shall behold
Beauty's self, that grows not old.

Night Lyric

In the world's far edges
Faint and blue,
Where the rocky ledges
Stand in view,

Fades the rosy, tender
Evening light;
Then in starry splendor
Comes the night.

So a stormy lifetime
Comes to close,
Spirit's mortal strifetime
Finds repose.

Faith and toil and vision
Crowned at last,
Failure and derision

Overpast,—

All the daylight splendor
Far above,
Calm and sure and tender
Comes thy love.

The Heart of Night

When all the stars are sown
Across the night-blue space,
With the immense unknown,
In silence face to face.

We stand in speechless awe
While Beauty marches by,
And wonder at the Law
Which wears such majesty.

How small a thing is man
In all that world-sown vast,
That he should hope or plan
Or dream his dream could last!

O doubter of the light,
Confused by fear and wrong,
Lean on the heart of night
And let love make thee strong!

The Good that is the True
Is clothed with Beauty still.
Lo, in their tent of blue,
The stars above the hill!

Peace

The sleeping tarn is dark
Below the wooded hill.
Save for its homing sounds,
The twilit world grows still.

And I am left to muse
In grave-eyed mystery,
And watch the stars come out

As sandalled dusk goes by.

And now the light is gone,
The drowsy murmurs cease,
And through the still unknown
I wonder whence comes peace.

Then softly falls the word
Of one beyond a name,
"Peace only comes to him
Who guards his life from shame,—

"Who gives his heart to love,
And holding truth for guide,
Girds him with fearless strength,
That freedom may abide."

The Old Gray Wall

Time out of mind I have stood
Fronting the frost and the sun,
That the dream of the world might endure,
And the goodly will be done.

Did the hand of the builder guess,
As he laid me stone by stone,
A heart in the granite lurked,
Patient and fond as his own?

Lovers have leaned on me
Under the summer moon,
And mowers laughed in my shade
In the harvest heat at noon.

Children roving the fields
With early flowers in spring,
Old men turning to look,
When they heard a bluebird sing,

Have seen me a thousand times
Standing here in the sun,
Yet never a moment dreamed
Whose likeness they gazed upon.

Ah, when will ye understand,
Mortals who strive and plod,—

Who rests on this old gray wall
Lays a hand on the shoulder of God!

Te Deum

If I could paint you the autumn color, the melting glow upon all things laid,
The violet haze of Indian summer, before its splendor begins to fade,
When scarlet has reached its breathless moment, and gold the hush of its glory now,
That were a mightier craft than Titian's, the heart to lift and the head to bow.

I should be lord of a world of rapture, master of magic and gladness, too,—
The touch of wonder transcending science, the solace escaping from line and hue;
I would reveal through tint and texture the very soul of this earth of ours,
Forever yearning through boundless beauty to exalt the spirit with all her powers.

See where it lies by the lake this morning, our autumn hillside of hardwood trees,
A masterpiece of the mighty painter who works in the primal mysteries.
A living tapestry, rich and glowing with blended marvels, vermilion and dun,
Hung out for the pageant of time that passes along an avenue of the sun!

The crown of the ash is tinged with purple, the hickory leaves are Etruscan gold,
And the tulip-tree lifts yellow banners against the blue for a signal bold;
The oaks in crimson cohorts stand, a myriad sumach torches mass
In festal pomp and victorious pride, when the vision of spring is brought to pass.

Down from the line of the shore's deep shadows another and softer picture lies,
As if the soul of the lake in slumber should harbor a dream of paradise,—
Passive and blurred and unsubstantial, lulling the sense and luring the mind
With the spell of an empty fairy world, where sinew and sap are left behind.

So men dream of a far-off heaven of power and knowledge and endless joy,
Asleep to the moment's fine elation, dull to the day's divine employ,
Musing over a phantom image, born of fantastic hope and fear,
Of the very happiness life engenders and earth provides—our privilege here.

Dare we dispel a single transport, neglect the worth that is here and now,
Yet dream of enjoying its shadowy semblance in the by-and-by somewhere, somehow?
I heard the wind on the hillside whisper, "They ill prepare for a journey hence
Who waste the senses and starve the spirit in a world all made for spirit and sense.

"Is the full stream fed from a stifled source, or the ripe fruit filled from a blighted flower?
Are not the brook and the blossom greatened through many a busy beatified hour?
Not in the shadow but in the substance, plastic and potent at our command,
Are all the wisdom and gladness of heart; this is the kingdom of heaven at hand."

So I will pass through the lovely world, and partake of beauty to feed my soul.

With earth my domain and growth my portion, how should I sue for a further dole?
In the lift I feel of immortal rapture, in the flying glimpse I gain of truth,
Released is the passion that sought perfection, assuaged the ardor of dreamful youth.

The patience of time shall teach me courage, the strength of the sun shall lend me poise.
I would give thanks for the autumn glory, for the teaching of earth and all her joys.
Her fine fruition shall well suffice me; the air shall stir in my veins like wine;
While the moment waits and the wonder deepens, my life shall merge with the life divine.

In October

Now come the rosy dogwoods,
The golden tulip-tree,
And the scarlet yellow maple,
To make a day for me.

The ash-trees on the ridges,
The alders in the swamp,
Put on their red and purple
To join the autumn pomp.

The woodbine hangs her crimson
Along the pasture wall,
And all the bannered sumacs
Have heard the frosty call.

Who then so dead to valor
As not to raise a cheer,
When all the woods are marching
In triumph of the year?

By Still Waters

"He leadeth me beside the still waters; He restoreth my soul."

"My tent stands in a garden
Of aster and goldenrod,
Tilled by the rain and the sunshine,
And sown by the hand of God,—
An old New England pasture
Abandoned to peace and time,
And by the magic of beauty
Reclaimed to the sublime.

About it are golden woodlands
Of tulip and hickory;
On the open ridge behind it
You may mount to a glimpse of sea,—
The far-off, blue, Homeric
Rim of the world's great shield,
A border of boundless glamor
For the soul's familiar field.

In purple and gray-wrought lichen
The boulders lie in the sun;
Along its grassy footpath
The white-tailed rabbits run.
The crickets work and chirrup
Through the still afternoon;
And the owl calls from the hillside
Under the frosty moon.

The odorous wild grape clambers
Over the tumbling wall,
And through the autumnal quiet
The chestnuts open and fall.
Sharing time's freshness and fragrance,
Part of the earth's great soul,
Here man's spirit may ripen
To wisdom serene and whole.

Shall we not grow with the asters—
Never reluctant nor sad,
Not counting the cost of being,
Living to dare and be glad?
Shall we not lift with the crickets
A chorus of ready cheer,
Braving the frost of oblivion,
Quick to be happy here?

Is my will as sweet as the wild grape,
Spreading delight on the air
For the passer-by's enchantment,
Subtle and unaware?
Have I as brave a spirit,
Sprung from the self-same mould,
As this weed from its own contentment
Lifting its shaft of gold?

The deep red cones of the sumach
And the woodbine's crimson's sprays
Have bannered the common roadside

For the pageant of passing days.
These are the oracles Nature
Fills with her holy breath,
Giving them glory of color,
Transcending the shadow of death.

Here in the sifted sunlight
A spirit seems to brood
On the beauty and worth of being,
In tranquil, instinctive mood;
And the heart, filled full of gladness
Such as the wise earth knows,
Wells with a full thanksgiving
For the gifts that life bestows:

For the ancient and virile nurture
Of the teeming primordial ground,
For the splendid gospel of color,
The rapt revelations of sound;
For the morning-blue above us
And the rusted gold of the fern,
For the chickadee's call of valor
Bidding the faint-heart turn;

For fire and running water,
Snowfall and summer rain;
For sunsets and quiet meadows,
The fruit and the standing grain;
For the solemn hour of moonrise
Over the crest of trees,
When the mellow lights are kindled
In the lamps of the centuries;

For those who wrought aforetime,
Led by the mystic strain
To strive for the larger freedom,
And live for the greater gain;
For plenty of peace and playtime,
The homely goods of earth,
And for rare immaterial treasures
Accounted of little worth;

For art and learning and friendship,
Where beneficent truth is supreme,—
Those everlasting cities
Built on the hills of dream;
For all things growing and goodly
That foster this life, and breed

The immortal flower of wisdom
Out of the mortal seed.

But most of all for the spirit
That cannot rest nor bide
In stale and sterile convenience,
Nor safety proven and tried,
But still inspired and driven,
Must seek what better may be,
And up from the loveliest garden
Must climb for a glimpse of sea.

Lines for a Picture

When the leaves are flying
Across the azure sky,
Autumn on the hill top
Turns to say good-by;

In her gold-red tunic,
Like an Eastern queen,
With untarnished courage
In her wilding mien.

All the earth below her
Answers to her gaze,
And her eyes are pensive
With remembered days.

Yet, with cheek ensanguined,
Gay at heart she goes
On the great adventure
Where the north wind blows.

The Deserted Pasture

I love the stony pasture
That no one else will have.
The old gray rocks so friendly seem,
So durable and brave.

In tranquil contemplation
It watches through the year.
Seeing the frosty stars arise,

The slender moons appear.

Its music is the rain-wind,
Its choristers the birds,
And there are secrets in its heart
Too wonderful for words.

It keeps the bright-eyed creatures
That play about its walls,
Though long ago its milking herds
Were banished from their stalls.

Only the children come there,
For buttercups in May,
Or nuts in autumn, where it lies
Dreaming the hours away.

Long since its strength was given
To making good increase,
And now its soul is turned again
To beauty and to peace.

There in the early springtime
The violets are blue,
And adder-tongues in coats of gold
Are garmented anew.

There bayberry and aster
Are crowded on its floors,
When marching summer halts to praise
The Lord of Out-of-doors.

And there October passes
In gorgeous livery,—
In purple ash, and crimson oak,
And golden tulip tree.

And when the winds of winter
Their bugle blasts begin,
The snowy hosts of heaven arrive
And pitch their tents therein.

Autumn

Now when the time of fruit and grain is come,
When apples hang above the orchard wall,

And from the tangle by the roadside stream
A scent of wild grapes fills the racy air,
Comes Autumn with her sunburnt caravan,
Like a long gypsy train with trappings gay
And tattered colors of the Orient,
Moving slow-footed through the dreamy hills.
The woods of Wilton at her coming wear
Tints of Bokhara and of Samarcand:
The maples glow with their Pompeian red,
The hickories with burnt Etruscan gold;
And while the crickets fife along her march,
Behind her banners burns the crimson sun.

November Twilight

Now Winter at the end of day
Along the ridges takes her way,

Upon her twilight round to light
The faithful candles of the night.

As quiet as the nun she goes
With silver lamp in hand, to close

The silent doors of dusk that keep
The hours of memory and sleep.

She pauses to tread out the fires
Where Autumn's festal train retires.

The last red embers smoulder down
Behind the steeples of the town.

Austere and fine the trees stand bare
And moveless in the frosty air,

Against the pure and paling light
Before the threshold of the night.

On purple valley and dim wood
The timeless hush of solitude

Is laid, as if the time for some
Transcending mystery were come,

That shall illumine and console

The penitent and eager soul,

Setting her free to stand before
Supernal beauty and adore.

Dear Heart, in heaven's high portico
It is the hour of prayer. And lo,

Above the earth, serene and still,
One star—our star—o'er Lonetree Hill!

The Ghost-yard of the Goldenrod

When the first silent frost has trod
The ghost-yard of the goldenrod,

And laid the blight of his cold hand
Upon the warm autumnal land,

And all things wait the subtle change
That men call death, is it not strange

That I—without a care or need,
Who only am an idle weed—

Should wait unmoved, so frail, so bold,
The coming of the final cold!

Before the Snow

Now soon, ah, very soon, I know
The trumpets of the north will blow,
And the great winds will come to bring
The pale, wild riders of the snow.

Darkening the sun with level flight,
At arrowy speed, they will alight,
Unnumbered as the desert sands,
To bivouac on the edge of night.

Then I, within their somber ring,
Shall hear a voice that seems to sing,
Deep, deep within my tranquil heart,
The valiant prophecy of spring.

Winter

When winter comes along the river line
And Earth has put away her green attire,
With all the pomp of her autumnal pride,
The world is made a sanctuary old,
Where Gothic trees uphold the arch of gray,
And gaunt stone fences on the ridge's crest
Stand like carved screens before a crimson shrine,
Showing the sunset glory through the chinks.
There, like a nun with frosty breath, the soul,
Uplift in adoration, sees the world
Transfigured to a temple of her Lord;
While down the soft blue-shadowed aisles of snow
Night, like a sacristan with silent step,
Passes to light the tapers of the stars.

A Winter Piece

Over the rim of a lacquered bowl,
Where a cold blue water-color stands,
I see the wintry breakers roll
And heave their froth up the freezing sands.

Here in immunity safe and dull,
Soul treads her circuit of trivial things.
There soul's brother, a shining gull,
Dares the rough weather on dauntless wings.

Winter Streams

Now the little rivers go
Muffled safely under snow,

And the winding meadow streams
Murmur in their wintry dreams,

While a tinkling music wells
Faintly from there icy bells,

Telling how their hearts are bold

Though the very sun be cold.

Ah, but wait until the rain
Comes a-sighing once again,

Sweeping softly from the Sound
Over ridge and meadow ground!

Then the little streams will hear
April calling far and near,—

Slip their snowy bands and run
Sparkling in the welcome sun.

Winter Twilight

Along the wintry skyline,
Crowning the rocky crest,
Stands the bare screen of hardwood trees
Against the saffron west,—
Its gray and purple network
Of branching tracery
Outspread upon the lucent air,
Like weed within the sea.

The scarlet robe of autumn
Renounced and put away,
The mystic Earth is fairer still,—
A Puritan in gray.
The spirit of the winter,
How tender, how austere!
Yet all the ardor of the spring
And summer's dream are here.

Fear not, O timid lover,
The touch of frost and rime!
This is the virtue that sustained
The roses in their prime.
The anthem of the northwind
Shall hallow thy despair,
The benediction of the snow
Be answer to thy prayer.

And now the star of evening
That is the pilgrim's sign,
Is lighted in the primrose dusk,—

A lamp before a shrine.
Peace fills the mighty minster,
Tranquil and gray and old,
And all the chancel of the west
Is bright with paling gold.

A little wind goes sifting
Along the meadow floor,—
Like steps of lovely penitents
Who sighingly adore.
Then falls the twilight curtain,
And fades the eerie light,
And frost and silence turn the keys
In the great doors of night.

The Twelfth Night Star

It is the bitter time of year
When iron is the ground,
With hasp and sheathing of black ice
The forest lakes are bound,
The world lies snugly under snow,
Asleep without a sound.

All the night long in trooping squares
The sentry stars go by,
The silent and unwearying hosts
That bear man company,
And with their pure enkindling fires
Keep vigils lone and high.

Through the dead hours before the dawn,
When the frost snaps the sill,
From chestnut-wooded ridge to sea
The earth lies dark and still,
Till one great silver planet shines
Above the eastern hill.

It is the star of Gabriel,
The herald of the Word
In days when messengers of God
With sons of men conferred,
Who brought the tidings of great joy
The watching shepherds heard;

The mystic light that moved to lead

The wise of long ago,
Out of the great East where they dreamed
Of truths they could not know,
To seek some good that should assuage
The world's most ancient woe.

O well, believe, they loved their dream,
Those children of the star,
Who saw the light and followed it,
Prophetical, afar,—
Brave Caspar, clear-eyed Melchior,
And eager Balthasar.

Another year slips to the void,
And still with omen bright
Above the sleeping doubting world
The day-star is alight,—
The waking signal flashed of old
In the blue Syrian night.

But who are now as wise as they
Whose faith could read the sign
Of the three gifts that shall suffice
To honor the divine,
And show the tread of common life
Ineffably benign?

Whoever wakens on a day
Happy to know and be,
To enjoy the air, to love his kind,
To labor, to be free,—
Already his enraptured soul
Lives in eternity.

For him with every rising sun
The year begins anew;
The fertile earth receives her lord,
And prophecy comes true,
Wondrously as a fall of snow,
Dear as a drench of dew.

Who gives his life for beauty's need,
King Caspar could no more;
Who serves the truth with single mind
Shall stand with Melchior;
And love is all that Balthasar
In crested censer bore.

A Christmas Eve Choral

Halleluja!
What sound is this across the dark
While all the earth is sleeping? Hark!
Halleluja! Halleluja! Halleluja!

Why are thy tender eyes so bright,
Mary, Mary?
On the prophetic deep of night
Joseph, Joseph,
I see the borders of the light,
And in the day that is to be
An aureoled man-child I see,
Great love's son, Joseph.

Halleluja!
He hears not, but she hears afar,
The Minstrel Angel of the star.
Halleluja! Halleluja! Halleluja!

Why is thy gentle smile so deep,
Mary, Mary?
It is the secret I must keep,
Joseph, Joseph,—
The joy that will not let me sleep,
The glory of the coming days,
When all the world shall turn to praise
God's goodness, Joseph.

Halleluja!
Clear as the bird that brings the morn
She hears the heavenly music borne.
Halleluja! Halleluja! Halleluja!

Why is thy radiant face so calm,
Mary, Mary?
His strength is like a royal palm,
Joseph, Joseph;
His beauty like the victor's psalm.
He moves like morning o'er the lands
And there is healing in his hands
For sorrow, Joseph.

Halleluja!
Tender as dew-fall on the earth

She hears the choral of love's birth.
Halleluja! Halleluja! Halleluja!

What is the message come to thee,
Mary, Mary?
I hear like wind within the tree,
Joseph, Joseph,
Or like a far-off melody
His deathless voice proclaiming peace,
And bidding ruthless wrong to cease,
For love's sake, Joseph.

Halleluja!
Moving as rain-wind in the spring
She hears the angel chorus ring.
Halleluja! Halleluja! Halleluja!

Why are thy patient hands so still,
Mary, Mary?
I see the shadow on the hill,
Joseph, Joseph,
And wonder if it is God's will
That courage, service, and glad youth
Shall perish in the cause of truth
Forever, Joseph.

Halleluja!
Her heart in that celestial chime
Has heard the harmony of time.
Halleluja! Halleluja! Halleluja!

Why is thy voice so strange and far,
Mary, Mary?
I see the glory of the star,
Joseph, Joseph;
And in its light all things that are,
Made glad and wise beyond the sway
Of death and darkness and dismay,
In God's time Joseph.

Halleluja!
To every heart in love 'tis given
To hear the ecstasy of heaven.
Halleluja! Halleluja! Halleluja.

Christmas Song

Above the weary waiting world,
Asleep in chill despair,
There breaks a sound of joyous bells
Upon the frosted air.
And o'er the humblest rooftree, lo,
A star is dancing on the snow.

What makes the yellow star to dance
Upon the brink of night?
What makes the breaking dawn to glow
So magically bright,—
And all the earth to be renewed
With infinite beatitude?

The singing bells, the throbbing star,
The sunbeams on the snow,
And the awakening heart that leaps
New ecstasy to know,—
They all are dancing in the morn
Because a little child is born.

The Wise Men from the East

(A LITTLE BOY'S CHRISTMAS LESSON)

Why were the Wise Men three,
Instead of five or seven?"
They had to match, you see,
The archangels in Heaven.

God sent them, sure and swift,
By his mysterious presage,
To bear the threefold gift
And take the threefold message.

Thus in their hands were seen
The gold of purest Beauty,
The myrrh of Truth all-clean,
The frankincense of Duty.

And thus they bore away
The loving heart's great treasure,
And knowledge clear as day,
To be our life's new measure.

They went back to the East
To spread the news of gladness.
There one became a priest
To the new word of sadness;

And one a workman, skilled
Beyond the old earth's fashion;
And one a scholar, filled
With learning's endless passion.

God sent them for a sign
He would not change nor alter
His good and fair design,
However man may falter.

He meant that, as He chose
His perfect plan and willed it,
They stood in place of those
Who elsewhere had fulfilled it;

Whoso would mark and reach
The height of man's election,
Must still achieve and teach
The triplicate perfection.

For since the world was made,
One thing was needed ever,
To keep man undismayed
Through failure and endeavor—

A faultless trinity
Of body, mind, and spirit,
And each with its own three
Strong angels to be near it;

Strength to arise and go
Wherever dawn is breaking,
Poise like the tides that flow,
Instinct for beauty-making;

Imagination bold
To cross the mystic border,
Reason to seek and hold,
Judgment for law and order;

Joy that makes all things well,
Faith that is all-availing
Each terror to dispel,

And Love, ah, Love unfailing.

These are the flaming Nine
Who walk the world unsleeping,
Sent forth by the Divine
With manhood in their keeping.

These are the seraphs strong
His mighty soul had need of,
When He would right the wrong
And sorrow He took heed of.

And that, I think, is why
The Wise Men knelt before Him,
And put their kingdoms by
To serve Him and adore Him;

So that our Lord, unknown,
Should not be unattended,
When He was here alone
And poor and unbefriended;

That still He might have three
(Rather than five or seven)
To stand in their degree,
Like archangels in Heaven.

The Sending of the Magi

In a far Eastern country
It happened long of yore,
Where a lone and level sunrise
Flushes the desert floor,
That three kings sat together
And a spearman kept the door.

Caspar, whose wealth was counted
By city and caravan;
With Melchior, the seer
Who read the starry plan;
And Balthasar, the blameless,
Who loved his fellow man.

There while they talked, a sudden
Strange rushing sound arose,
And as with startled faces

They thought upon their foes,
Three figures stood before them
In imperial repose.

One in flame-gold and one in blue
And one in scarlet clear,
With the almighty portent
Of sunrise they drew near!
And the kings made obeisance
With hand on breast, in fear.

"Arise," said they, "we bring you
Good tidings of great peace!
To-day a power is wakened
Whose working must increase,
Till fear and greed and malice
And violence shall cease."

The messengers were Michael,
By whom all things are wrought
To shape and hue; and Gabriel
Who is the lord of thought;
And Rafael without whose love
All toil must come to nought.

Then Rafael said to Balthasar,
"In a country west from here
A lord is born in lowliness,
In love without a peer.
Take grievances and gifts to him
And prove his kingship clear!

"By this sign ye shall know him;
Within his mother's arm
Among the sweet-breathed cattle
He slumbers without harm,
While wicked hearts are troubled
And tyrants take alarm."

And Gabriel said to Melchior,
"My comrade, I will send
My star to go before you,
That ye may comprehend
Where leads your mystic learning
In a humaner trend."

And Michael said to Gaspar,
"Thou royal builder, go

With tribute of thy riches!
Though time shall overthrow
Thy kingdom, no undoing
His gentle might shall know."

Then while the kings' hearts greatened
And all the chamber shone,
As when the hills at sundown
Take a new glory on
And the air thrills with purple,
Their visitors were gone.

Then straightway up rose Gaspar,
Melchior and Balthasar,
And passed out through the murmur
Of palace and bazar,
To make without misgiving
The journey of the Star.

The Angels of Man

The word of the Lord of the outer worlds
Went forth on the deeps of space,
That Michael, Gabriel, Rafael,
Should stand before his face,
The seraphs of his threefold will,
Each in his ordered place.

Brave Michael, the right hand of God,
Strong Gabriel, his voice,
Fair Rafael, his holy breath
That makes the world rejoice,—
Archangels of omnipotence,
Of knowledge, and of choice;

Michael, angel of loveliness
In all things that survive,
And Gabriel, whose part it is
To ponder and contrive,
And Rafael, who puts the heart
In every thing alive.

Came Rafael, the enraptured soul,
Stainless as wind or fire,
The urge within the flux of things,
The life that must aspire,

With whom is the beginning,
The worth, and the desire;

And Gabriel, the all-seeing mind,
Bringer of truth and light,
Who lays the courses of the stars
In their stupendous flight,
And calls the migrant flocks of spring
Across the purple night;

And Michael, the artificer
Of beauty, shape, and hue,
Lord of the forges of the sun,
The crucible of the dew,
And driver of the plowing rain
When the flowers are born anew.

Then said the Lord: "Ye shall account
For the ministry ye hold,
Since ye have been my sons to keep
My purpose from of old.
How fare the realms within your sway
To perfections still untold?"

Answered each as he had the word.
And a great silence fell
On all the listening hosts of heaven
To hear their captains tell,—
With the breath of the wind, the call of a bird.
And the cry of a mighty bell.

Then the Lord said: "The time is ripe
For finishing my plan,
And the accomplishment of that
For which all time began.
Therefore on you is laid the task
Of the fashioning of man;

"In your own likeness shall he be,
To triumph in the end.
I only give him Michael's strength
To guard him and defend,
With Gabriel to be his guide,
And Rafael his friend.

"Ye shall go forth upon the earth,
And make there Paradise,
And be the angels of that place

To make men glad and wise,
With loving-kindness in their hearts,
And knowledge in their eyes.

"And ye shall be man's counsellors
That neither rest nor sleep,
To cheer the lonely, lift the frail,
And solace them that weep.
And ever on his wandering trail
Your watch-fires ye shall keep;

"Till in the far years he shall find
The country of his quest,
The empire of the open truth,
The vision of the best,
Foreseen by every mother saint
With her new-born on her breast."

At the Making of Man

First all the host of Raphael
In liveries of gold,
Lifted the chorus on whose rhythm
The spinning spheres are rolled,—
The Seraphs of the morning calm
Whose hearts are never cold.

He shall be born a spirit,
Part of the soul that yearns,
The core of vital gladness
That suffers and discerns,
The stir that breaks the budding sheath
When the green spring returns,—

The gist of power and patience
Hid in the plasmic clay,
The calm behind the senses,
The passionate essay
To make his wise and lovely dream
Immortal on a day.

The soft, Aprilian ardors
That warm the waiting loam
Shall whisper in his pulses
To bid him overcome,
And he shall learn the wonder-cry

Beneath the azure dome.

And though all-dying nature
Should teach him to deplore,
The ruddy fires of autumn
Shall lure him but the more
To pass from joy to stronger joy,
As through an open door.

He shall have hope and honor,
Proud trust and courage stark,
To hold him to his purpose
Through the unlighted dark,
And love that sees the moon's full orb
In the first silver arc.

And he shall live by kindness
And the heart's certitude,
Which moves without misgiving
In ways not understood,
Sure only of the vast event,—
The large and simple good.

Then Gabriel's host in silver gear
And vesture twilight blue,
The spirits of immortal mind,
The warders of the true,
Took up the theme that gives the world
Significance anew.

He shall be born to reason,
And have the primal need
To understand and follow
Wherever truth may lead,—
To grow in wisdom like a tree
Unfolding from a seed.

A watcher by the sheepfolds,
With wonder in his eyes,
He shall behold the seasons,
And mark the planets rise,
Till all the marching firmament
Shall rouse his vast surmise.

Beyond the sweep of vision,
Or utmost reach of sound,
This cunning fire-maker,
This tiller of the ground,

Shall learn the secrets of the suns
And fathom the profound.

For he must prove all being
Sane, beauteous, benign,
And at the heart of nature
Discover the divine,—
Himself the type and symbol
Of the eternal trine.

He shall perceive the kindling
Of knowledge, far and dim,
As of the fire that brightens
Below the dark sea-rim,
When ray by ray the splendid sun
Floats to the world's wide brim.

And out of primal instinct,
The lore of lair and den,
He shall emerge to question
How, wherefore, whence, and when,
Till the last frontier of the truth
Shall lie within his ken.

Then Michael's scarlet-suited host
Took up the word and sang;
As though a trumpet had been loosed
In heaven, the arches rang;
For these were they who feel the thrill
Of beauty like a pang.

He shall be framed and balanced
For loveliness and power,
Lithe as the supple creatures,
And colored as a flower,
Sustained by the all-feeding earth,
Nurtured by wind and shower,

To stand within the vortex
Where surging forces play,
A poised and pliant figure
Immutable as they,
Till time and space and energy
Surrenders to his sway.

He shall be free to journey
Over the teeming earth,
An insatiable seeker,

A wanderer from his birth,
Clothed in the fragile veil of sense,
With fortitude for girth.

His hands shall have dominion
Of all created things,
To fashion in the likeness
Of his imaginings,
To make his will and thought survive
Unto a thousand springs.

The world shall be his province,
The princedom of his skill;
The tides shall wear his harness,
The winds obey his will;
Till neither flood, nor fire, nor frost,
Shall work to do him ill.

A creature fit to carry
The pure creative fire,
Whatever truth inform him,
Whatever good inspire,
He shall make lovely in all things
To the end of his desire.

St. Michael's Star

In the pure solitude of dusk
One star is set to shine
Above the sundown's dying rose,
A lamp before a shrine.
It is the star of Michael lit
In the minster of the sun,
That every toiling hand may give
Thanks for the day's work done.

For when the almighty word went forth
To bid creation be,—
The glimmering star-tracks on the blue,
The tide-belts on the sea,—
Perfect as planned, from Michael's hand
The lasting hills arose,
Their bases on the poppied plain,
Their peaks in bannered snows.

Cedar and thorn and oak were born;

Green fiddleheads uncurled
In the spring woods; gold adder-tongues
Came forth to glad the world;—
The magic of the punctual seeds,
Each with its pregnant powers,
As the lord Michael fashioned them
To keep their days and hours.

Frail fins to ride the monstrous tide,
Soft wings to poise and gleam,
He formed the pageant tribe by tribe
As vivid as a dream.
And still must his beneficence
Renew, create, sustain,
Sorcery of the wind and sun,
Alchemy of the rain.

Teeming with God, the kindly sod
Yearns through the summer days
With the mute eloquence of flowers,
Its only means of praise.
At dusk and dawn the tranquil hills
Throb to the song of birds,
And all the dim blue silence thrills
To transport not of words.

For earth must breed to spirit's need,
Clay to the finer clay,
That soul through sense find recompense
And rapture on her way.
And man, from dust and dreaming wrought,
To all things must impart
The trend and likeness of his thought,
The passion of his heart.

The love and lore he shall acquire
To word and deed must dare;
Resemblances of God his sire
His voice and mien must bear.
His children's children shall portray
The skill which he bestows
On living; and what life must mean
His craftsman's instinct knows.

Line upon line and tone by tone,
The visioned form he gives
To sound and color, wood and stone,
Takes loveliness and lives.

He sees his project's soaring hope
Grow substance, and expand
To measure a diviner scope
Beneath his patient hand.

To pencil, brush, and burnisher
His wizardry he lends,
And to the care of lathe and loom
His secret he commends.
In hues and forms and cadences
New beauty he instills,
A brother by the right of craft
To Michael of the hills.

The Dreamers

Charlemagne with knight and lord,
In the hill at Ingelheim,
Slumbers at the council board,
Seated waiting for the time.

With their swords across their knees
In that chamber dimly lit,
Chin on breast life effigies
Of the dreaming gods, they sit.

Long ago they went to sleep,
While great wars above them hurled.
Taking counsel how to keep
Giant evil from the world.

Golden-armored, iron-crowned,
There in silence they await
The last war,—in war renowned,
Done with doubting and debate.

What is all our clamor for?
Petty virtue, puny crime,
Beat in vain against the door
Of the hill at Ingelheim.

When at last shall dawn the day
For the saving of the world,
They will forth in war array,
Iron-armored, golden-curled.

In the hill at Ingelheim,
Still, they say, the Emperor,
Like a warrior in his prime,
Waits the message at the door.

Shall the long enduring fight
Break above our heads in vain,
Plunged in lethargy and night,
Like the men of Charlemagne?

Comrades, through the Council Hall
Of the heart, inert and dumb,
Hear ye not the summoning call,
"Up, my lords, the hour is come!"

El Dorado

This is the story
Of Santo Domingo,
The first established
Permanent city
Built in the New World.

Miguel Dias,
A Spanish sailor
In the fleet of Columbus,
Fought with a captain,
Wounded him, then in fear
Fled from his punishment.

Ranging the wilds, he came
On a secluded
Indian village
Of the peace-loving
Comely Caguisas.
There he found shelter,
Food, fire, and hiding,—
Welcome unstinted.

Over this tribe ruled—
No cunning chieftain
Grown gray in world-craft,
But a young soft-eyed
Girl, tender-hearted,
Loving, and regal
Only in beauty,

With no suspicion
Of the perfidious
Merciless gold-lust
Of the white sea-wolves,—
Roving, rapacious,
Conquerors, destroyers.
Strongly the stranger
Wooed with his foreign
Manners, his Latin
Fervor and graces;
Beat down her gentle,
Unreserved strangeness;

Made himself consort
Of a young queen, all
Loveliness, ardor,
And generous devotion.
Her world she gave him,
Nothing denied him,
All, all for love's sake
Poured out before him,—
Lived but to pleasure
And worship her lover.

Such is the way
Of free-hearted women,
Radiant beings
Who carry God's secret;
All their seraphic
Unworldly wisdom
Spent without fearing
Or calculation
For the enrichment
Of—whom, what, and wherefore?

Ask why the sun shines
And is not measured,
Ask why the rain falls
Aeon by aeon,
Ask why the wind comes
Making the strong trees
Blossom in springtime,
Forever unwearied!
Whoever earned these gifts,
Air, sun, and water?
Whoever earned his share
In that unfathomed
Full benediction,

Passing the old earth's
Cunningest knowledge,
Greater than all
The ambition of ages,
Light as a thistle-seed,
Strong as a tide-run,
Vast and mysterious
As the night sky,—
The love of woman?
Not long did Miguel
Dias abide content
With his good fortune.
Back to his voyaging
Turned his desire,
Restless once more to rove
With boon companions,
Filled with the covetous
Thirst for adventure,—
The white man's folly.

Then poor Zamcaca,
In consternation
Lest she lack merit
Worthy to tether
His wayward fancy,
Knowing no way but love,
Guileless, and sedulous
Only to gladden,
Quick and sweet-souled
As another madonna,
Gave him the secret
Of her realm's treasure,—
Raw gold unweighed,
Stored wealth unimagined;
Decked him with trappings
Of that yellow peril;
And bade him go
Bring his comrades to settle
In her dominion.

Not long the Spaniards
Stood on that bidding.
Gold was their madness,
Their Siren and Pandar.
Trooping they followed
Their friend the explorer,
Greed-fevered ravagers

Of all things goodly,
Hot-foot to plunder
The land of his love-dream.
They swooped on that country,
Founded their city,
Made Miguel Dias
Its first Alcalde,—
Flattered and fooled him,
Loud in false praises
For the great wealth he had
By his love's bounty.

Then the old story,
Older than Adam,—
Treachery, rapine,
Ingratitude, bloodshed,
Wrought by the strong man
On unsuspecting
And gentler brothers.
The rabid Spaniard,
Christian and ruthless
(Like any modern
Magnate of Mammon),
Harried that fearless,
Light-hearted, trustful folk
Under his booted heel.
Tears (ah, a woman's tears,—
The grief of angels,—)
Fell from Zamcaca,
Sorrowing, hopeless,
Alone, for her people.

Sick from injustice,
Distraught, and disheartened,
Tortured by sight and sound
Of wrong and ruin,
When the kind, silent,
Tropical moonlight,
Lay on the city,
In the dead hour
When the soul trembles
Within the portals
Of its own province,
While far away seem

All deeds of daytime,
She rose and wondered;
Gazed on the sleeping

Face of her loved one,
Alien and cruel;
Kissed her strange children,
Longingly laying a hand
In farewell on each,
Crept to the door, and fled
Back to the forest.

Only the deep heart
Of the World-mother,
Brooding below the storms
Of human madness,
Can know what desolate
Anguish possessed her.

Only the far mind
Of the World-father,
Seeing the mystic
End and beginning,
Knows why the pageant
Is so betattered
With mortal sorrow.

On the Plaza

One August day I sat beside
A café window open wide
To let the shower-freshened air
Blow in across the Plaza, where
In golden pomp against the dark
Green leafy background of the Park,
St. Gaudens' hero, gaunt and grim,
Rides on with Victory leading him.

The wet, black asphalt seemed to hold
In every hollow pools of gold,
And clouds of gold and pink and gray
Were piled up at the end of day,
Far down the cross street, where one tower
Still glistened from the drenching shower.

A weary, white-haired man went by,
Cooling his forehead gratefully
After the day's great heat. A girl,
Her thin white garments in a swirl
Blown back against her breasts and knees,

Like a Winged Victory in the breeze,
Alive and modern and superb,
Crossed from the circle of the curb.

We sat there watching people pass,
Clinking the ice against the glass
And talking idly—books or art,
Or something equally apart
From the essential stress and strife
That rudely form and further life,
Glad of a respite from the heat,
When down the middle of the street,
Trundling a hurdy-gurdy, gay
In spite of the dull-stifling day,
Three street-musicians came. The man,
With hair and beard as black as Pan,
Strolled on one side with lordly grace,
While a young girl tugged at a trace
Upon the other. And between
The shafts there walked a laughing queen,
Bright as a poppy, strong and free.
What likelier land than Italy
Breeds such abandon? Confident
And rapturous in mere living spent
Each moment to the utmost, there
With broad, deep chest and kerchiefed hair,
With head thrown back, bare throat, and waist
Supple, heroic and free-laced,
Between her two companions walked
This splendid woman, chaffed and talked,
Did half the work, made all the cheer
Of that small company.

No fear
Of failure in a soul like hers
That every moment throbs and stirs
With merry ardor, virile hope,
Brave effort, nor in all its scope
Has room for thought or discontent,
Each day its own sufficient vent
And source of happiness.

Without
A trace of bitterness or doubt
Of life's true worth, she strode at ease
Before those empty palaces,
A simple heiress of the earth
And all its joys by happy birth,

Beneficent as breeze or dew,
And fresh as though the world were new
And toil and grief were not. How rare
A personality was there!

A Painter's Holiday

We painters sometimes strangely keep
These holidays. When life runs deep
And broad and strong, it comes to make
Its own bright-colored almanack.
Impulse and incident divine
Must find their way through tone and line;
The throb of color and the dream
Of beauty, giving art its theme
From dear life's daily miracle,
Illume the artist's life as well.
A bird-note, or a turning leaf,
The first white fall of snow, a brief
Wild song from the Anthology,
A smile, or a girl's kindling eye,—
And there is worth enough for him
To make the page of history dim.
Who knows upon what day may come
The touch of that delirium
Which lifts plain life to the divine,
And teaches hand the magic line
No cunning rule could ever reach,
Where Soul's necessities find speech?
None knows how rapture may arrive
To be our helper, and survive
Through our essay to help in turn
All starving eager souls who yearn
Lightward discouraged and distraught.
Ah, once art's gleam of glory caught
And treasured in the heart, how then
We walk enchanted among men,
And with the elder gods confer!
So art is hope's interpreter,
And with devotion must conspire
To fan the eternal altar fire.
Wherefore you find me here to-day,
Not idling the good hours away,
But picturing a magic hour
With its replenishment of power.

Conceive a bleak December day,
The streets all mire, the sky all gray,
And a poor painter trudging home
Disconsolate, when what should come
Across his vision, but a line
On a bold-lettered play-house sign,
A Persian Sun Dance.

In he turns.
A step, and there the desert burns
Purple and splendid; molten gold
The streamers of the dawn unfold,
Amber and amethyst uphurled
Above the far rim of the world;
The long-held sound of temple bells
Over the hot sand steals and swells;
A lazy tom-tom throbs and dones
In barbarous maddening monotones;
While sandal incense blue and keen
Hangs in the air. And then the scene
Wakes, and out steps, by rhythm released,
The sorcery of all the East,
In rose and saffron gossamer,—
A young light-hearted worshipper
Who dances up the sun. She moves
Like waking woodland flower that loves
To greet the day. Her lithe, brown curve
Is like a sapling's sway and swerve
Before the spring wind. Her dark hair
Framing a face vivid and rare,
Curled to her throat and then flew wild,
Like shadows round a radiant child.
The sunlight from her cymbals played
About her dancing knees, and made
A world of rose-lit ecstasy,
Prophetic of the day to be.

Such mystic beauty might have shone
In Sardis or in Babylon,
To bring a Satrap to his doom
Or touch some lad with glory's bloom.
And now it wrought for me, with sheer
Enchantment of the dying year,
Its irresistible reprieve
From joylessness on New Year's Eve.

Mirage

Here hangs at last, you see, my row
Of sketches,—all I have to show
Of one enchanted summer spent
In sweet laborious content,
At little 'Sconset by the moors,
With the sea thundering by its doors,
Its grassy streets, and gardens gay
With hollyhocks and salvia.

And here upon the easel yet,
With the last brush of paint still wet,
(Showing how inspiration toils),
Is one where the white surf-line boils
Along the sand, and the whole sea
Lifts to the skyline, just to be
The wondrous background from whose verge
Of blue on blue there should emerge
This miracle.

One day of days
I strolled the silent path that strays
Between the moorlands and the beach
From Siasconset, till you reach
Tom Nevers Head, the lone last land
That fronts the ocean, lone and grand
As when the Lord first bade it be
For a surprise and mystery.
A sailless sea, a cloudless sky,
The level lonely moors, and I
The only soul in all that vast
Of color made intense to last!
The small white sea-birds piping near;
The great soft moor-winds; and the dear
Bright sun that pales each crest to jade,
Where gulls glint fishing unafraid.

Here man, the godlike, might have gone
With his deep thought, on that wild dawn
When the first sun came from the sea,
Glowing and kindling the world to be,
While time began and joy had birth,—
No wilder sweeter spot on earth!

As I sat there and mused (the way
We painters waste our time, you say!)
On the sheer loneliness and strength

Whence life must spring, there came at length
Conviction of the helplessness
Of earth alone to ban or bless.
I saw the huge unhuman sea;
I heard the drear monotony
Of the waves beating on the shore
With heedless, futile strife and roar,
Without a meaning or an aim.

And then a revelation came,
In subtle, sudden, lovely guise,
Like one of those soft mysteries
Of Indian jugglers, who evoke
A flower for you out of smoke.
I knew sheer beauty without soul
Could never be perfection's goal,
Nor satisfy the seeking mind
With all it longs for and must find
One day. The lovely things that haunt
Our senses with an aching want,
And move our souls, are like the fair
Lost garments of a soul somewhere.
Nature is naught, if not the veil
Of some great good that must prevail
And break in joy, as woods of spring
Break into song and blossoming.

But what makes that great goodness start
Within ourselves? When leaps the heart
With gladness, only then we know
Why lovely Nature travails so,—
Why art must persevere and pray
In her incomparable way.
In all the world the only worth
Is human happiness; its dearth
The darkest ill. Let joyance be,
And there is God's sufficiency,—
Such joy as only can abound
Where the heart's comrade has been found.

That was my thought. And then the sea
Broke in upon my revery
With clamorous beauty,—the superb
Eternal noun that takes no verb
But love. The heaven of dove-like blue
Bent o'er the azure, round and true
As magic sphere of crystal glass,
Where faith sees plain the pageant pass

Of things unseen. So I beheld
The sheer sky-arches domed and belled,
As if the sea were the very floor
Of heaven where walked the gods of yore
In Plato's imagery, and I
Uplifted saw their pomps go by.

The House of space and time grew tense
As if with rapture's imminence,
When truth should be at last made clear,
And the great worth of life appear;
While I, a worshipper at the shrine,
For very longing grew divine,
Borne upward on earth's ecstasy,
And welcomed by the boundless sky.

A mighty prescience seemed to brood
Over that tenuous solitude
Yearning for form, till it became
Vivid as dream and live as flame,
Through magic art could never match,
The vision I have tried to catch,—
All earth's delight and meaning grown
A lyric presence loved and known.

How otherwise could time evolve
Young courage, or the high resolve,
Or gladness to assuage and bless
The soul's austere great loneliness,
Than by providing her somehow
With sympathy of hand and brow,
And bidding her at last go free,
Companioned through eternity?

So there appeared before my eyes,
In a beloved, familiar guise,
A vivid, questing human face
In profile, scanning heaven for grace,
Up-gazing there against the blue
With eyes that heaven itself shone through;
The lips soft-parted, half in prayer,
Half confident of kindness there;
A brow like Plato's made for dream
In some immortal Academe,
And tender as a happy girl's;
A full dark head of clustered curls
Round as an emperor's, where meet
Repose and ardor, strong and sweet,

Distilling from a mind unmarred
The glory of her rapt regard.

So eager Mary might have stood,
In love's adoring attitude,
And looked into the angel's eyes
With faith and fearlessness, all wise
In soul's unfaltering innocence,
Sure in her woman's supersense
Of things only the humble know.
My vision looks forever so.

In other years when men shall say,
"What was the painter's meaning, pray?
Why all this vast of sea and space,
Just to enframe a woman's face?"
Here is the pertinent reply,
"What better use for earth and sky?"

The great archangel passed that way
Illuming life with mystic ray.
Not Lippo's self nor Raphael
Had lovelier, realer things to tell
Than I, beholding far away
How all the melting rose and gray
Upon the purple sea-line leaned
About that head that intervened.

How real was she? Ah, my friend,
In art the fact and fancy blend
Past telling. All the painter's task
Is with the glory. Need we ask
The tulips breaking through the mould
To their untarnished age of gold,
Whence their ideals were derived
That have so gloriously survived?
Flowers and painters both must give
The hint they have received, to live,—
Spend without stint the joy and power
That lurk in each propitious hour,—
Yet leave the why untold—God's way.

My sketch is all I have to say.

The Winged Victory

Thou dear and most high Victory,
Whose home is the unvanquished sea,
Whose fluttering wind-blown garments keep
The very freshness, fold, and sweep
They wore upon the galley's prow,
By what unwonted favor now
Hast thou alighted in this place,
Thou Victory of Samothrace?

O thou to whom in countless lands
With eager hearts and striving hands
Strong men in their last need have prayed,
Greatly desiring, undismayed,
And thou hast been across the fight
Their consolation and their might,
Withhold not now one dearer grace,
Thou Victory of Samothrace!

Behold, we, too, must cry to thee,
Who wage our strife with Destiny,
And give for Beauty and for Truth
Our love, our valor and our youth.
Are there no honors for these things
To match the pageantries of kings?
Are we more laggard in the race
Than those who fell at Samothrace?

Not only for the bow and sword,
O Victory, be thy reward!
The hands that work with paint and clay
In Beauty's service, shall not they
Also with mighty faith prevail?
Let hope not die, nor courage fail,
But joy come with thee pace for pace,
As once long since in Samothrace.

Grant us the skill to shape the form
And spread the color living-warm,
(As they who wrought aforetime did),
Where love and wisdom shall lie hid,
In fair impassioned types, to sway
The cohorts of the world to-day,
In Truth's eternal cause, and trace
Thy glory down from Samothrace.

With all the ease and splendid poise
Of one who triumphs without noise,
Wilt thou not teach us to attain

Thy sense of power without strain,
That we a little may possess
Our souls with thy sure loveliness,—
That calm the years cannot deface,
Thou Victory of Samothrace?

Then in the ancient, ceaseless war
With infamy, go thou before!
Amid the shoutings and the drums
Let it be learned that Beauty comes,
Man's matchless Paladin to be,
Whose rule shall make his spirit free
As thine from all things mean or base,
Thou Victory of Samothrace.

The Gate of Peace

Ah, who will build the city of our dream,
Where beauty shall abound and truth avail,
With patient love that is too wise for strife,
Blending in power as gentle as the rain
With the reviving earth on full spring days?
Who now will speed us to its gate of peace,
And reassure us on our doubtful road?

Three centuries ago a fearless man,
Yearning to set his people in the way,
Threw all his royal might into a plan
To found an ideal city that should give
Freedom to every instinct for the best,
From humblest impulse in his own domain
To rumored wisdom from the world's far ends.
Strengthened with ardor from a high resolve,
Beneath the patient smile of Indian skies
This fair dream flourished for a score of years,
Until the blight of evil touched its bloom
With fading, and transformed its vivid life
Into a ghost-flower of its fair design.

Now ruined nursery tower and gay boudoir,
A sad custodian of sacred tombs,
And scattered feathers from the purple wings
Of doves who reign in undisputed calm
Over this Eden of hope and fair essay,
Recall the valor of this ancient quest.

Great Akbar,—grandfather of Shah Jehan,
The artist Emperor of India
Who built the Taj for love of one held dear
Beyond all other women in the world,
And left that loveliest memorial,
The most supreme of wonders wrought by man,
To move for very joy all hearts to tears
Beholding how great beauty springs from love,—
Akbar the wisest ruler over Ind,
Grandson of Babar in whose veins were mixed
The blood of Tamerlane and Chinghiz Khan,
Who beat the Afghans and the Rajputs down
At Paniput and Buxar in Bengal,
Making himself the lord of Hindustan,
And with his restless Tartars founded there
The Mogul empire with its Moslem faith,
Its joyousness, enlightenment, and art,—
Akbar of all the sovereigns of the East
Is still most deeply loved and gladly praised.

For he who conquered with so strong a hand
Cabul, Kashmir, and Kandahar, and Sind,
Oudh and Orissa, Chitor and Ajmir,
With all their wealth to weld them into one,
Upholding justice with his sovereignty
Throughout his borders and imposing peace,
Was first and last a seeker after truth.

No craven unlaborious truce he sought,
But that great peace which only comes with light,
Emerging after chaos has been quelled
In some long struggle of enduring will,
To be a proof of order and of law,
Which cannot rest on falsehood nor on wrong,
But spreads like generous sunshine on the earth
When goodness has been gained and truth made clear,
At whatsoe'er incalculable cost.
Returning once with his victorious arms
And war-worn companies on the homeward march
To Agra and his court's magnificence,
From a campaign against some turbulent folk,
He came at evening to a quiet place
Near Sikri by the roadside through the woods,
Where there were many doves among the trees.

There Salim Chisti a holy man had made
His lonely dwelling in the wilderness,
Seeking perfection. And the solitude

Was sweet to Akbar, and he halted there
And went to Salim in his lodge and said,
"O man and brother, thy long days are spent
In meditation, seeking for the path
Through this great world's impediments to peace,
Here in the twilight with the holy stars
Or when the rose of morning breaks in gold;
Tell me, I pray, whence comes the gift of peace
With all its blessings for a people's need,
And how may true tranquillity be found
On which man's restless spirit longs to rest?"

And Salim answered, "Lord, most readily
In Allah's out-of-doors, for there men live
More truly, being free from false constraint,
For learning wisdom with a calmer mind.
For they who would find peace must conquer fear
And ignorance and greed,—the ravagers
Of spirit, mind, and sense,—and learn to live
Content beneath the shade of Allah's hand.
Who worships not his own will shall find peace."

Then Akbar answered, "I have set my heart
On making beauty, truth, and justice shine
As the ordered stars above the darkened earth.
Are not these also things to be desired,
And striven for with no uncertain toil?
And save through them whence comes the gift of peace?"

Then Salim smiled, and with his finger drew
In the soft dust before his door, and said,
"O king, thy words are true, thy heart most wise.
Thou also shalt find peace, as Allah wills,
Through following bravely what to thee seems best.
When any question, 'What is peace?' reply,
'The shelter of the Gate of Paradise,
The shadow of the archway, not the arch,
Within whose shade at need the poor may rest,
The weary be refreshed, the weak secure,
And all men pause to gladden as they go.'"

And Akbar pondered Salim Chisti's words.
Then turning to his ministers, he said,
"Here will I build my capital, and here
The world shall come unto a council hall,
And in a place of peace pursue the quest
Of wisdom and the finding out of truth,
That there be no more discord upon earth,

But only knowledge, beauty, and good will."

And it was done according to Akbar's word.
There in the wilderness as by magic rose
Futtehpur Sikri, the victorious city,
Of marble and red sandstone among the trees,
A rose unfolding in the kindling dawn.
Palace and mosque and garden and serai,
Bazaars and baths and spacious pleasure grounds,
By favor of Allah to perfection sprang.

Thus Akbar wrought to make his dream come true.
From the four corners of the world he brought
His master workmen, from Iran and Ind,
From wild Mongolia and the Arabian wastes;
Masons from Bagdad, Delhi, and Multan;
Dome builders from the North, from Samarkand;
Cunning mosaic workers from Kanauj;
And carvers of inscriptions from Shiraz;
And they all labored with endearing skill,
Each at his handicraft, to make beauty be.

When the first ax-blade on the timber rang,
The timid doves, as if foreboding ill,
Had fled from Sikri and its quiet groves.

But as he promised, Akbar sent and bade
The wise men of all nations to his court,
Brahman and Christian, Buddhist and Parsee,
Jain and stiff Mohammedan and Jew,
All followers of the One with many names,
Bringing the ghostly wisdom of the earth.

And so they came of every hue and creed.
From the twelve winds of heaven their caravans
Drew into Sikri as Akbar summoned them,
To spend long afternoons in council grave,
Sifting tradition for the seed of truth,
In the great mosque in Futtehpur at peace.
And Salim Chisti lived his holy life,
Beloved and honored there as Akbar's friend.

But light and changeable are the hearts of men.
Soon in that city dedicate to peace
Dissensions spread and rivalries grew rife,
Envy and bitterness and strife returned
Once more, and truth before them fled away.
Then Salim Chisti, coming to Akbar spoke,

"Lord, give thy servant leave now to depart
And follow where the fluttered wings have gone,
For here there is no longer any peace,
And truth cannot prevail where discord dwells."

"Nay then," said Akbar, "'tis not thou but I
Who am the servant here and must go hence.
I found thee master of this solitude,
Lord of the princedom of a quiet mind,
A sovereign vested in tranquillity,
And I have done thee wrong and stayed thy feet
From following perfection, with my horde
Of turbulent malcontents; and my loved dream
To build a city of abiding peace
Was but a vain illusion. Therefore now
This foolish people shall be driven forth
From this fair place, to live as they may choose
In disputance and wrangling longer still,
Until they learn, if Allah wills it so,
To lay aside their folly for the truth."

And as the king commanded, so it was.
More quickly than he came, with all his court
And hosts of followers he went away,
Leaving the place to solitude once more,—
A rose to wither where it once had blown.

To-day the all-kind unpolluted sun
Shines through the marble fret-work with no sound;
The winds play hide and seek through corridors
Where stately women with dark glowing eyes
Have laughed and frolicked in their fluttering robes;
The rose leaves drop with none to gather them,
In gardens where no footfall comes with eve,
Nor any lovers watch the rising moon;
And ancient silence, truer than all speech,
Still holds the secrets of the Council Hall,
Upon whose walls frescoes of many faiths
Attest the courtesy of open minds.

Before the last camp-follower was gone,
The doves returned and took up their abode
In the main gate of those deserted walls.
And in their custody this "Gate of Peace"
Bears still the grandeur of its origin,
Firing anew the wistful hearts of men
To brave endeavor with replenished hope,
Though since that time three hundred years ago,

The magic hush of those forsaken streets
And empty courtyards has been undisturbed
Save by the gentle whirring of grey wings,
With cooing murmurs uttered all day long,
And reverent tread of those from near and far,
Who still pursue the immemorial quest.

Epilogue

When all my writing has been done
Except the final colophon,

And I must bid beloved verse
Farewell for better or for worse,

Let me not linger o'er the page
In doubting and regretful age;

But as an unknown scribe in some
Monastic dim scriptorium,

When twilight on his labour fell
At the glad-heard refection bell,

Might add poor Body's thanks to be
From spiritual toils set free,

Let me conclude with hearty zest
Laus Deo! Nunc bibendum est!

Bliss Carman - An Appreciation

How many Canadians—how many even among the few who seek to keep themselves informed of the best in contemporary literature, who are ever on the alert for the new voices—realise, or even suspect, that this Northern land of theirs has produced a poet of whom it may be affirmed with confidence and assurance that he is of the great succession of English poets? Yet such—strange and unbelievable though it may seem—is in very truth the case, that poet being (to give him his full name) William Bliss Carman. Canada has full right to be proud of her poets, a small body though they are; but not only does Mr. Carman stand high and clear above them all—his place (and time cannot but confirm and justify the assertion) is among those men whose poetry is the shining glory of that great English literature which is our common heritage.

If any should ask why, if what has been just said is so, there has been—as must be admitted—no general recognition of the fact in the poet's home land, I would answer that there are various and plausible, if not good, reasons for it.

First of all, the poet, as thousands more of our young men of ambition and confidence have done, went early to the United States, and until recently, except for rare and brief visits to his old home down by the sea, has never returned to Canada—though for all that, I am able to state, on his own authority, he is still a Canadian citizen. Then all his books have had their original publication in the United States, and while a few of them have subsequently carried the imprints of Canadian publishers, none of these can be said ever to have made any special effort to push their sale. Another reason for the fact above mentioned is that Mr. Carman has always scorned to advertise himself, while his work has never been the subject of the log-rolling and booming which the work of many another poet has had—to his ultimate loss. A further reason is that he follows a rule of his own in preparing his books for publication. Most poets publish a volume of their work as soon as, through their industry and perseverance, they have material enough on hand to make publication desirable in their eyes. Not so with Mr. Carman, however, his rule being not to publish until he has done sufficient work of a certain general character or key to make a volume. As a result, you cannot fully know or estimate his work by one book, or two books, or even half a dozen; you must possess or be familiar with every one of the score and more volumes which contain his output of poetry before you can realise how great and how many-sided is his genius.

It is a common remark on the part of those who respond readily to the vigorous work of Kipling, or Masefield, even our own Service, that Bliss Carman's poetry has no relation to or concern with ordinary, everyday life. One would suppose that most persons who cared for poetry at all turned to it as a relief from or counter to the burdens and vexations of the daily round; but in any event, the remark referred to seems to me to indicate either the most casual acquaintance with Mr. Carman's work, or a complete misunderstanding and misapprehension of the meaning of it. I grant that you will find little or nothing in it all to remind you of the grim realities and vexing social problems of this modern existence of ours; but to say or to suggest that these things do not exist for Mr. Carman is to say or to suggest something which is the reverse of true. The truth is, he is aware of them as only one with the sensitive organism of a poet can be; but he does not feel that he has a call or mission to remedy them, and still less to sing of them. He therefore leaves the immediate problems of the day to those who choose, or are led, to occupy themselves therewith, and turns resolutely away to dwell upon those things which for him possess infinitely greater importance.

"What are they?" one who knows Mr. Carman only as, say, a lyrist of spring or as a singer of the delights of vagabondia probably will ask in some wonder. Well, the things which concern him above all, I would answer, are first, and naturally, the beauty and wonder of this world of ours, and next the mystery of the earthly pilgrimage of the human soul out of eternity and back into it again.

The poems in the present volume—which, by the way, can boast the high honor of being the very first regular Canadian edition of his work—will be evidence ample and conclusive to every reader, I am sure, of the place which

The perennial enchanted
Lovely world and all its lore

occupy in the heart and soul of Bliss Carman, as well as of the magical power with which he is able to convey the deep and unfailing satisfaction and delight which they possess for him. They, however, represent his latest period (he has had three well-defined periods), comprising selections from three of his last published volumes: The Rough Rider, Echoes from Vagabondia, and April Airs, together with a number of new poems, and do not show, except here and there and by hints and flashes, how great is his preoccupation with the problem of man's existence—

—the hidden import
Of man's eternal plight.

This is manifest most in certain of his earlier books, for in these he turns and returns to the greatest of all the problems of man almost constantly, probing, with consummate and almost unrivalled use of the art of expression, for the secret which surely, he clearly feels, lies hidden somewhere, to be discovered if one could but pierce deeply enough. Pick up Behind the Arras, and as you turn over page after page you cannot but observe how incessantly the poet's mind—like the minds of his two great masters, Browning and Whitman—works at this problem. In "Behind the Arras," the title poem; "In the Wings," "The Crimson House," "The Lodger," "Beyond the Gamut," "The Juggler"—yes, in every poem in the book—he takes up and handles the strange thing we know as, or call, life, turning it now this way, now that, in an effort to find out its meaning and purpose. He comes but little nearer success in this than do most of the rest of men, of course; but the magical and ever-fresh beauty of his expression, the haunting melody of his lines, the variety of his images and figures and the depth and range of his thought, put his searchings and ponderings in a class by themselves.

Lengthy quotation from Mr. Carman's books is not permitted here, and I must guide myself accordingly, though with reluctance, because I believe that in a study such as this the subject should be allowed to speak for himself as much as possible. In "Behind the Arras" the poet describes the passage from life to death as

A cadence dying down unto its source
In music's course,

and goes on to speak of death as

—the broken rhythm of thought and man,
The sweep and span
Of memory and hope
About the orbit where they still must grope
For wider scope,

To be through thousand springs restored, renewed,
With love imbrued,
With increments of will
Made strong, perceiving unattainment still
From each new skill.

Now follow some verses from "Behind the Gamut," to my mind the poet's greatest single achievement;

As fine sand spread on a disc of silver,

At some chord which bids the motes combine,
Heeding the hidden and reverberant impulse,
Shifts and dances into curve and line,

The round earth, too, haply, like a dust-mote,
Was set whirling her assigned sure way,
Round this little orb of her ecliptic
To some harmony she must obey.

And what of man?

Linked to all his half-accomplished fellows,
Through unfrontiered provinces to range—
Man is but the morning dream of nature,
Roused to some wild cadence weird and strange.

Here, now, are some verses from "Pulvis et Umbra," which is to be found in Mr. Carman's first book, Low Tide on Grand Pré, and in which the poet addresses a moth which a storm has blown into his window:

For man walks the world with mourning
Down to death and leaves no trace,
With the dust upon his forehead,
And the shadow on his face.

Pillared dust and fleeing shadow
As the roadside wind goes by,
And the fourscore years that vanish
In the twinkling of an eye.

"Pillared dust and fleeing shadow." Where in all our English literature will one find the life history of man summed up more briefly and, at the same time, more beautifully, than in that wonderful line? Now follows a companion verse to those just quoted, taken from "Lord of My Heart's Elation," which stands in the forefront of From the Green Book of the Bards. It may be remarked here that while the poet recurs again and again to some favorite thought or idea, it is never in the same words. His expression is always new and fresh, showing how deep and true is his inspiration. Again it is man who is pictured:

A fleet and shadowy column
Of dust and mountain rain,
To walk the earth a moment
And be dissolved again.

But while Mr. Carman's speculations upon life's meaning and the mystery of the future cannot but appeal to the thoughtful-minded, it is as an interpreter of nature that he makes his widest appeal. Bliss Carman, I must say here, and emphatically, is no mere landscape-painter; he never, or scarcely ever, paints a picture of nature for its own sake. He goes beyond the outward aspect of things and interprets or translates for us with less keen senses as only a poet whose feeling for nature is of the deepest and profoundest, who has gone to her whole-heartedly and been taken close to her warm bosom, can do. Is this not evident from these verses from "The Great Return"—originally called "The Pagan's Prayer," and for some inscrutable reason to be found only in the limited Collected Poems, issued in two stately volumes in 1905.

When I have lifted up my heart to thee,
Thou hast ever hearkened and drawn near,
And bowed thy shining face close over me,
Till I could hear thee as the hill-flowers hear.

When I have cried to thee in lonely need,
Being but a child of thine bereft and wrung,
Then all the rivers in the hills gave heed;
And the great hill-winds in thy holy tongue—

That ancient incommunicable speech—
The April stars and autumn sunsets know—
Soothed me and calmed with solace beyond reach
Of human ken, mysterious and low.

Who can read or listen to those moving lines without feeling that Mr. Carman is in very truth a poet of nature—nay, Nature's own poet? But how could he be other when, in "The Breath of the Reed" (From the Green Book of the Bards), he makes the appeal?

Make me thy priest, O Mother,
And prophet of thy mood,
With all the forest wonder
Enraptured and imbued.

As becomes such a poet, and particularly a poet whose birth-month is April, Mr. Carman sings much of the early spring. Again and again he takes up his woodland pipe, and lo! Pan himself and all his train troop joyously before us. Yet the singer's notes for all his singing never become wearied or strident; his airs are ever new and fresh; his latest songs are no less spontaneous and winning than were his first, written how many years ago, while at the same time they have gained in beauty and melody. What heart will not stir to the vibrant music of his immortal "Spring Song," which was originally published in the first Songs from Vagabondia, and the opening verses of which follow?

Make me over, mother April,
When the sap begins to stir!
When thy flowery hand delivers
All the mountain-prisoned rivers,
And thy great heart beats and quivers
To revive the days that were,
Make me over, mother April,
When the sap begins to stir!

Take my dust and all my dreaming,
Count my heart-beats one by one,
Send them where the winters perish;
Then some golden noon recherish

And restore them in the sun,
Flower and scent and dust and dreaming,
With their heart-beats every one!

That poem is sufficient in itself to prove that Bliss Carman has full right and title to be called Spring's own lyrist, though it may be remarked here that not all his spring poems are so unfeignedly joyous. Many of them indeed, have a touch, or more than a touch, of wistfulness, for the poet knows well that sorrow lurks under all joy, deep and well hidden though it may be.

Mr. Carman sings equally finely, though perhaps not so frequently, of summer and the other seasons; but as he has other claims upon our attention, I shall forbear to labor the fact, particularly as the following collection demonstrates it sufficiently. One of those other claims is as a writer of sea poetry. Few poets, it may be said, have pictured the majesty and the mystery, the beauty and the terror of the sea, better than he. His Ballads of Lost Haven is a veritable treasure-house for those whose spirits find kinship in wide expanses of moving waters. One of the best known poems in this volume is "The Gravedigger," which opens thus:

Oh, the shambling sea is a sexton old,
And well his work is done.
With an equal grave for lord and knave,
He buries them every one.

Then hoy and rip, with a rolling hip,
He makes for the nearest shore;
And God, who sent him a thousand ship,
Will send him a thousand more;
But some he'll save for a bleaching grave,
And shoulder them in to shore—
Shoulder them in, shoulder them in,
Shoulder them in to shore.

In "The City of the Sea" (Last Songs from Vagabondia) Mr. Carman speaks of the seabells sounding

The eternal cadence of sea sorrow
For Man's lot and immemorial wrong—
The lost strains that haunt the human dwelling
With the ghost of song.

Elsewhere he speaks of

The great sea, mystic and musical.

And here from another poem is a striking picture:

... the old sea
Seems to whimper and deplore
Mourning like a childless crone
With her sorrow left alone—

The eternal human cry
To the heedless passer-by.

I have said above that Mr. Carman has had three distinct periods, and intimated that the poems in the following collection are of his third period. The first period may be said to be represented by the Low Tide and Behind the Arras volumes, while the second is displayed in the three volumes of Songs from Vagabondia, which he published in association with his friend Richard Hovey. Bliss Carman was from the first too original and individual a poet to be directly influenced by anyone else; but there can be no doubt that his friendship with Hovey helped to turn him from over-preoccupation with mysteries which, for all their greatness, are not for man to solve, to an intenser realisation of the beauty and loveliness of the world about him and of the joys of human fellowship. The result is seen in such poems as "Spring Song," quoted in part above, and his perhaps equally well-known "The Joys of the Road," which appeared in the same volume with that poem, and a few verses from which follow:

Now the joys of the road are chiefly these:
A crimson touch on the hardwood trees;

A vagrant's morning wide and blue,
In early fall, when the wind walks, too;

A shadowy highway cool and brown,
Alluring up and enticing down

From rippled waters and dappled swamp,
From purple glory to scarlet pomp;

The outward eye, the quiet will,
And the striding heart from hill to hill.

Some of the finest of arman's work is contained in his elegiac or memorial poems, in which he commemorates Keats, Shelley, William Blake, Lincoln, Stevenson, and other men for whom he has a kindred feeling, and also friends whom he has loved and lost. Listen to these moving lines from "Non Omnis Moriar," written in memory of Gleeson White, and to be found in Last Songs from Vagabondia:

There is a part of me that knows,
Beneath incertitude and fear,
I shall not perish when I pass
Beyond mortality's frontier;

But greatly having joyed and grieved,
Greatly content, shall hear the sigh
Of the strange wind across the lone
Bright lands of taciturnity.

In patience therefore I await
My friend's unchanged benign regard,—
Some April when I too shall be
Spilt water from a broken shard.

In "The White Gull," written for the centenary of the birth of Shelley in 1892, and included in By the Aurelian Wall, he thus apostrophizes that clear and shining spirit:

O captain of the rebel host,
Lead forth and far!
Thy toiling troopers of the night
Press on the unavailing fight;
The sombre field is not yet lost,
With thee for star.

Thy lips have set the hail and haste
Of clarions free
To bugle down the wintry verge
Of time forever, where the surge
Thunders and trembles on a waste
And open sea.

In "A Seamark," a threnody for Robert Louis Stevenson, which appears in the same volume, the poet hails "R.L.S." (of whose tribe he may be said to be truly one) as

The master of the roving kind,

and goes on:

O all you hearts about the world
In whom the truant gypsy blood,
Under the frost of this pale time,
Sleeps like the daring sap and flood
That dreams of April and reprieve!
You whom the haunted vision drives,
Incredulous of home and ease.
Perfection's lovers all your lives!

You whom the wander-spirit loves
To lead by some forgotten clue
Forever vanishing beyond
Horizon brinks forever new;
Our restless loved adventurer,
On secret orders come to him,
Has slipped his cable, cleared the reef,
And melted on the white sea-rim.

"Perfection's lovers all your lives." Of these, it may be said without qualification, is Bliss Carman himself.

No summary of Mr. Carman's work, however cursory, would be worthy of the name if it omitted mention of his ventures in the realm of Greek myth. From the Book of Myths is made up of work of that sort, every poem in it being full of the beauty of phrase and melody of which Mr. Carman alone has the secret. The finest poems in the book, barring the opening one, "Overlord," are "Daphne," "The Dead Faun," "Hylas," and "At Phædra's Tomb," but I can do no more here than name them, for extracts would fail to reveal their full beauty. And beauty, after all is said, is the first and last thing with Mr. Carman. As he says himself somewhere:

The joy of the hand that hews for beauty
Is the dearest solace under the sun.

And again

The eternal slaves of beauty
Are the masters of the world.

A slave—a happy, willing slave—to beauty is the poet himself, and the world can never repay him for the message of beauty which he has brought it.

Kindred to From the Book of Myths, but much more important, is Sappho: One Hundred Lyrics, one of the most successful of the numerous attempts which have been made to recapture the poems by that high priestess of song which remain to us only in fragments. Mr. Carman, as Charles G. D. Roberts points out in an introduction to the volume, has made no attempt here at translation or paraphrasing; his venture has been "the most perilous and most alluring in the whole field of poetry"—that of imaginative and, at the same time, interpretive construction. Brief quotation again would fail to convey an adequate idea of the exquisiteness of the work, and all I can do, therefore, is to urge all lovers of real poetry to possess themselves of Sappho: One Hundred Lyrics, for it is literally a storehouse of lyric beauty.

I must not fail here to speak of From the Book of Valentines, which contains some lovely things, notably "At the Great Release." This is not only one of the finest of all Mr. Carman's poems, but it is also one of the finest poems of our time. It is a love poem, and no one possessing any real feeling for poetry can read it without experiencing that strange thrill of the spirit which only the highest form of poetry can communicate. "Morning and Evening," "In an Iris Meadow," and "A letter from Lesbos" must be also mentioned. In the last named poem, Sappho is represented as writing to Gorgo, and expresses herself in these moving words:

If the high gods in that triumphant time
Have calendared no day for thee to come
Light-hearted to this doorway as of old,
Unmoved I shall behold their pomps go by—
The painted seasons in their pageantry,
The silvery progressions of the moon,
And all their infinite ardors unsubdued,
Pass with the wind replenishing the earth

Incredulous forever I must live
And, once thy lover, without joy behold,
The gradual uncounted years go by,
Sharing the bitterness of all things made.

Mention must be now made of Songs of the Sea Children, which can be described only as a collection of the sweetest and tenderest love lyrics written in our time—

—the lyric songs
The earthborn children sing,
When wild-wood laughter throngs
The shy bird-throats of spring;
When there's not a joy of the heart
But flies like a flag unfurled,
And the swelling buds bring back
The April of the world.

So perfect and complete are these lyrics that it would be almost sacrilege to quote any of them unless entire. Listen however, to these verses:

The day is lost without thee,
The night has not a star.
Thy going is an empty room
Whose door is left ajar.

Depart: it is the footfall
Of twilight on the hills.
Return: and every rood of ground
Breaks into daffodils.

There are those who will have it that Bliss Carman has been away from Canada so long that he has ceased to be, in a real sense, a Canadian. Such assume rather than know, for a very little study of his work would show them that it is shot through and through with the poet's feeling for the land of his birth. Memories of his childhood and youthful years down by the sea are still fresh in Mr. Carman's mind, and inspire him again and again in his writing. "A Remembrance," at the beginning of the present collection, may be pointed to as a striking instance of this, but proof positive is the volume, Songs from a Northern Garden, for it could have been written only by a Canadian, born and bred, one whose heart and soul thrill to the thought of Canada. I would single out from this volume for special mention as being "Canadian" in the fullest sense "In a Grand Pré Garden," "The Keeper's Silence," "At Home and Abroad," "Killoleet," and "Above the Gaspereau," but have no space to quote from them.

But Mr. Carman is not only a Canadian, he is also a Briton; and evidence of this is his Ode on the Coronation, written on the occasion of the crowning of King Edward VII in 1902. This poem—the very existence of which is hardly known among us—ought to be put in the hands of every child and youth who speaks the English tongue, for no other, I dare maintain—nothing by Kipling, or Newbolt, or any other of our so-called "Imperial singers"—expresses more truly and more movingly the deep feeling of love and reverence which the very thought of England evokes in every son of hers, even though it may never have been his to see her white cliffs rise or to tread her storied ground:

O England, little mother by the sleepless Northern tide,
Having bred so many nations to devotion, trust, and pride,
Very tenderly we turn
With welling hearts that yearn

Still to love you and defend you,—let the sons of men discern
Wherein your right and title, might and majesty, reside.

In concluding this, I greatly fear, lamentably inadequate study, I come to the collection which follows, and which, as intimated above, represents the work of Mr. Carman's latest period. I must say at once that, while I yield to no one in admiration for Low Tide and the other books of that period, or for the work of the second period, as represented by the Songs from Vagabondia volumes, I have no hesitation in declaring that I regard the poet's work of the past few years with even higher admiration. It may not possess the force and vigor of the work which preceded it; but anything seemingly missing in that respect is more than made up for me by increased beauty and clarity of expression. The mysticism—verging, or more than verging, at times on symbolism—which marked his earlier poems, and which hung, as it were, as a veil between them and the reader, has gone, and the poet's thought or theme now lies clearly before us as in a mirror. What—to take a verse from the following pages at random—could be more pellucid, more crystal clear in expression—what indeed, could come closer to that achieving of the impossible at which every real poet must aim—than this from "In Gold Lacquer".

Gold are the great trees overhead,
And gold the leaf-strewn grass,
As though a cloth of gold were spread
To let a seraph pass.
And where the pageant should go by,
Meadow and wood and stream,
The world is all of lacquered gold,
Expectant as a dream.

The poet, happily, has fully recovered from the serious illness which laid him low some two years ago, and which for a time caused his friends and admirers the gravest concern, and so we may look forward hopefully to seeing further volumes of verse come from the press to make certain his name and fame. But if, for any reason, this should not be—which the gods forfend!—Later Poems, I dare affirm, must and will be regarded as the fine flower and crowning achievement of the genius and art of Bliss Carman.

R. H. HATHAWAY.
Toronto, 1921.

Bliss Carman – A Short Biography

William Bliss Carman was born in Fredericton, in New Brunswick on April 15th 1861. 'Bliss' was his mother's maiden name. She was descended from Daniel Bliss of Concord, Massachusetts, who was the great-grandfather to Ralph Waldo Emerson.

Carman was educated at Fredericton Collegiate School. Here, under the influence of the headmaster George Robert Parkin, he gained an appreciation of classical literature and was introduced to the poetry of many of the Pre-Raphaelites especially Dante Gabriel Rossetti and Algernon Charles Swinburne.

From here he graduated to the University of New Brunswick, obtaining his B.A. there in 1881. As is common with so many writers his first published piece was for the University magazine and for Carman that was in 1879.

England now beckoned and he spent a year at Oxford and then the University of Edinburgh (1882–1883). He returned home to Canada to work on his M.A. which he obtained from the University of New Brunswick in 1884.

Tragically his father died in January, 1885, followed by his mother in February of the following year. Carman now enrolled in Harvard University for a year. There he met and was part of a literary circle that included the American poet Richard Hovey, who would become his close friend, and later collaborator, on the successful Vagabondia poetry series. Carman and Hovey were members of the "Visionists" circle along with Herbert Copeland and F. Holland Day, who would later form the Boston publishing firm Copeland & Day and, in turn, launch Vagabondia.

After Harvard Carman briefly returned to Canada, but was back in Boston by February of 1890 saying "Boston is one of the few places where my critical education and tastes could be of any use to me in earning money. New York and London are about the only other places." However, he was unable to find work in Boston but was more successful in New York becoming the literary editor of the semi-religious New York Independent. There he helped Canadian poets get published and introduced them to a wider readership than they could receive in Canada.

However, Carman and work as an editor were not destined for a long career together and he was dismissed in 1892. There followed short stays with Current Literature, Cosmopolitan, The Chap-Book, and The Atlantic Monthly. Whilst these appointments provided the basis for a career and an income he was not suited to their demands. From 1895 he would only work as a contributor to magazines and newspapers whilst he worked on his volumes of poetry.

Carman first published a book of poetry in 1893 with Low Tide on Grand Pré. He had written the title poem in the summer of 1886 and it had (whilst he was still at Harvard) been published in the spring of 1887 by Atlantic Monthly. Despite its critical acceptance there was no Canadian company prepared to publish the volume. When an American company did so it went bankrupt. Life was becoming difficult for the young poet.

The following year was decidedly better. His partnership with Richard Hovey had given birth to Songs of Vagabondia and it was published by their friends at Copeland & Day. It was an immediate success. The young men were delighted at such a reception. It quickly sold out and was re-printed a number of times. Although these re-prints were small (usually 500-1000 copies) they were frequent.

On the back of this success they would write a further three volumes, which in their turn were almost as successful. They quickly became the center of a cult following, especially among students who empathized with the poetry's anti-materialistic themes, its celebration of personal freedom, and its glorification of comradeship."

The success of Songs of Vagabondia prompted the Boston firm, Stone & Kimball, to reissue Low Tide on Grand Pré and to hire Carman as the editor of its literary journal, The Chapbook. This ceased after a year when the company relocated and Carman expressed his desire to remain in Boston.

In 1885 Carman brought out Behind the Arras, a somewhat more serious and philosophical work centered on the premise of a long meditation using the speaker's house and its many rooms as a symbol of life and the choices to be made. However, the idea and its execution did not quite meld.

Signficantly, in 1896, Carman met Mrs Mary Perry King, who rapidly became patron, adviser and sometime lover. She put money in his pocket, and food in his mouth and, when he struck bottom, often repaired his confidence as well as helping to sell the work. She also later became his writing collaborator on two verse dramas.

Mitchell Kennerley, Carman's roommate wrote that, "On the rare occasions they had intimate relations they always advised me of by leaving a bunch of violets — Mary favorite flower — on the pillow of my bed." If her husband, Dr. King, knew of this arrangement he seems not to have objected. He was a great supporter of Carman's career and seemingly his wife's complicated involvement with that.

In 1897 Carman published Ballad of Lost Haven, a collection of poetry about the sea. Its notable poems include the macabre sea shanty, The Gravedigger. The following year, 1898, came By the Aurelian Wall, the title poem itself was an elegy to John Keats and the book a collection of formal elegies.

In 1899 his publisher, Lamson, Wolffe was taken over by the Boston firm of Small, Maynard & Co., who had also acquired the rights to Low Tide on Grand Pré. The copyrights to of his books were now held by one publisher and, in lieu of earnings, Carman took what would ultimately be a disastrous financial stake in the company.

As the century turned Carman was hard at work on what would eventually be a five-volume set of poetry; "Pans Pipes". Pan, the goat-god, was traditionally associated with poetry and the coming together of the earthly and the divine. The five volumes were all published between 1902 – 1905.

The inspiration for this came from Mary who had persuaded Carman to write in both prose and poetry about the ideas of 'unitrinianism.' This drew on the theories of François-Alexandre-Nicolas-Chéri Delsarte and was defined as a strategy of mind-body-spirit harmonization aimed at undoing the physical, psychological, and spiritual damage caused by urban modernity. The definition may be rather woolly but for Carman it resulted in some very fine work across the five-volume series. This shared belief between Mary and Carman created a further bond but did isolate him from his circle of friends.

The excellence of a number of these poems did much to install Carman as the most noted of Canadian Poets and eventually their own Poet Laureate. Among the most often quoted and printed are "The Dead Faun" (from Volume I), "Lord of My Heart's Elation" (Volume II) and many of the erotic poems from Volume III.

In the middle of publication in 1903, Small, Maynard failed and with it went all the assets Carman had tied up in the company.

Carman immediately signed with another Boston publisher, L.C. Page, who would publish seven new books of Carman poetry in this hectic period up to 1905. They released a further three books based on Carman's Transcript columns, and a prose work on Unitrinianism, The Making of Personality, that he'd written with Mary King.

Carman now felt secure enough to pursue his 'dream project,' namely a deluxe edition of his collected poetry to 1903. Page acquired the distribution rights on the condition that the book be sold privately, by subscription. Unfortunately, the demand wasn't there and it failed. Carman was deeply disappointed and lost faith in Page. However, their grip on his copyrights was absolute and sadly no further collected editions were to be published during his lifetime.

By 1904 his income was restricted and the offer to be editor-in-chief of the 10-volume project, The World's Best Poetry, was eagerly accepted.

For Carman perhaps his best years as a poet were now behind him. From 1908 he lived near the Kings' New Canaan, Connecticut, estate, that he named "Sunshine", or in the summer in a cabin in the Catskills, which he called "Moonshine."

With Literary tastes now moving away from what he could provide his income further dwindled and his health started to deteriorate.

In 1912 Carman published the final work in the Vagabondia series. Richard Hovey had died in 1900 and so this last work was purely his. It has a distinct elegiac tone as if remembering the past works themselves.

Although Carman was not politically active he did campaign during the World War One, as a member of the Vigilantes, who supported the American entry into the titanic struggle on the Allied side.

By 1920, Carman was impoverished and recovering from a near-fatal attack of tuberculosis. He returned to Canada and began to undertake a series of publicly successful and somewhat lucrative reading tours, saying "there is nothing worth talking of in book sales compared with reading. Breathless attention, crowded halls, and a strange, profound enthusiasm such as I never guessed could be,' he reported to a friend. 'And good thrifty money too. Think of it! An entirely new life for me, and I am the most surprised person in Canada.'"

On October 28th, 1921 Carman was honored at a dinner held by the newly-formed Canadian Authors' Association, at the Ritz Carlton Hotel in Montreal, where he was crowned Canada's Poet Laureate with a wreath of maple leaves.

Carman is placed among the Confederation Poets, a group that included his cousin, Charles G.D. Roberts, Archibald Lampman, and Duncan Campbell Scott. Carman was perhaps the best and is credited with the widest recognition. However, whilst the others carefully supplemented their income with writing novels and works for the magazines, or even other careers, Carman only wrote poetry together with a small amount of writing on literary ideas, philosophy, and aesthetics.

He continued his reading tours, and by 1925 had finally secured a new Canadian publisher; McClelland & Stewart (Toronto), who issued a collection of selected earlier verse and would now became his main publisher. Although they benefited from Carman's increased popularity and his revered position in Canadian literature, his former publisher L.C. Page would not relinquish its copyrights to his earlier works.

In his last years, Carman was a member of the Halifax literary and social set, The Song Fishermen and in 1927 he edited The Oxford Book of American Verse.

William Bliss Carman died of a brain hemorrhage, at the age of 68, in New Canaan on the 8th June, 1929. He was cremated in New Canaan and his ashes interred at Forest Hill Cemetery, Fredericton, with a national memorial service held at the Anglican cathedral there.

It was only a quarter of a century later, on May 13th, 1954, that a scarlet maple tree was planted at his graveside, to honour his request in the 1892 poem "The Grave-Tree":

Let me have a scarlet maple
For the grave-tree at my head,
With the quiet sun behind it,
In the years when I am dead.

Bliss Carman – A Concise Bibliography

Poetry Collections
Low Tide on Grand Pre: A Book of Lyrics (1893)
Songs from Vagabondia (1894)
A Seamark: A Threnody for Robert Louis Stevenson (1895)
Behind the Arras: A Book of the Unseen (1895)
More Songs from Vagabondia (1896)
Ballads of Lost Haven: A Book of the Sea (1897)
By the Aurelian Wall: And Other Elegies (1898)
A Winter Holiday (1899)
Last Songs from Vagabondia (1901)
Ballads and Lyrics (1902)
Ode on the Coronation of King Edward (1902)
Pipes of Pan: From the Book of Myths (1902)
Pipes of Pan: From the Green Book of the Bards (1903)
Pipes of Pan: Songs of the Sea Children (1904)
Pipes of Pan: Songs from a Northern Garden (1904)
Pipes of Pan: From the Book of Valentines (1905)
Sappho: One Hundred Lyrics (1904)
Poems (1905)
The Rough Rider: And Other Poems (1909)
A Painter's Holiday, and Other Poems (1911)
Echoes from Vagabondia (1912)
April Airs: A Book of New England Lyrics (1916)
The Man of The Marne: And Other Poems (1918)
The Vengeance of Noel Brassard: A Tale of the Acadian Expulsion (1919)
Far Horizons (1925)
Later Poems (1926)
Sanctuary: Sunshine House Sonnets (1929)
Wild Garden (1929)
Bliss Carman's Poems (1931)

Drama
Bliss Carman & Mary Perry King. Daughters of Dawn: A Lyrical Pageant of a Series of Historical Scenes for Presentation with Music and Dancing (1913)
Bliss Carman & Mary Perry King. Earth Deities: And Other Rhythmic Masques (1914)

Prose Collections
The Kinship of Nature (1904)
The Poetry of Life (1905)
The Friendship of Art (1908)
The Making of Personality (1908)
Talks on Poetry and Life; Being a Series of Five Lectures Delivered Before the University of Toronto, December 1925 (Speech). transcribed by Blanche Hume. 1926.
Bliss Carman's Scrap-Book: A Table of Contents (Pierce, Lorne, editor) (1931)

Editor
The World's Best Poetry (10 volumes) (1904)
The Oxford Book of American Verse (U.S. editor) (1927)
Carman, Bliss; Pierce, Lorne, editors (1935). Our Canadian Literature: Representative Verse, English and French.

www.ingramcontent.com/pod-product-compliance
Lightning Source LLC
Chambersburg PA
CBHW061445040426
42450CB00007B/1216